# ...And Your
# Daughters Shall Preach

## DEVELOPING A FEMALE MENTORING PROGRAM
## IN THE AFRICAN AMERICAN CHURCH

HODALE PRESS, INC.
P.O. Box 5415
Saint Louis, Missouri 63147

---

### Library of Congress Cataloging-in-Publication Data

Lightner, A.F.
  And Your Daughters Shall Preach
  1. Preaching.  2. Mentorship Programs.  3. Self-Improvement
  I. Title.  II. Author.

ISBN 1-884594-10-7

---

50042895    Printed in the United States of America    4-6505

# Ann Farrar Lightner

## ...And Your Daughters Shall Preach

### DEVELOPING A FEMALE MENTORING PROGRAM IN THE AFRICAN AMERICAN CHURCH

Hodale Press, Inc.

P.O. Box 5415 - St. Louis, Mo. 63147

*To the Women in my Family*
*"Born in the Days When Hope Unborn had Died,"*
*Great-grandmother, Annamire West,*
*Grandmother, Hattie Rosetta Harris,*
*Mother, Brooksie Lee Harris Farrar.*
*To my beloved sister, Hattie Delores Farrar*
*Who Rejoices with me in the Miracles of God.*
*To the Women of Mt. Calvary A.M.E. Church,*
*Who Participated in this "Sisters Sharing" Group.*

# TABLE OF CONTENTS

# *FOREWORD*

African American women are born with two strikes against them: they are black and female in a country that is both racist and sexist. The popular culture feeds them a constant diet of negative images and negative messages. Where white women complain about a "glass ceiling," African American women live with a "SOLID STEEL" ceiling. (Some would even say they live with an 8-inch thick reinforced steel ceiling!)

African American women are told from the day they are born that they are ugly and hopelessly inferior; that they are un-blonde, non-white and highly expendable. They are sex objects, good for only one thing; and they will never be a Barbie or the CEO of a Fortune 500 company. They dare not dream of being the chairperson of any significant board. They can throw ministry out of their minds. Certain jobs—as well as church positions—are reserved for men-only!

Add to that already dismal scenario the pseudo-scholarship of a racist "Bell Curve" and you have the suffocating atmosphere into which every African American girl is born in the 20th (and approaching the 21st) Century. How then, can we expect to raise and nurture African queens like we once produced if this is the climate in which they are forced to exist? Where then does an African American women learn to affirm (or even *acknowledge*) her gifts?

In what setting—given the reality of the dominant culture and the sexist black church scene—can an African American woman use her God-given talents and abilities with no fear of being put down or kept in her place? Where can she "find (or use) her voice"? Where can she develop and grow spiritually, socially and mentally? Is there a place in the African American church where she can be all that she can be? Must African American women rely solely on male leadership in the African American Church?

It is these questions that Dr. Lightner addresses in this compelling and powerful book. The work grows out of a female mentoring program that Dr. Lightner designed to help African American church women overcome the obstacles faced simply by being born black and female. Lightner's program was implemented in the church where she pastors—the Mount Calvary A.M.E. Church—in Towson, Maryland.

Solidly based on the word of God, Lightner's process carries women through an examination of Scripture, the social contexts in which they live, and of their own spirituality in order to break the yokes that keep so many African American women bound! Most of the extant commentaries and Bible studies written in the African American community, are written from a male perspective and written by males themselves.

Lightner tackles this problem head-on by providing a 12-month Bible study program that emphasizes the female hermeneutic. She adds her own critical insights as a woman pastor and exegete. To give the study a deeper dimension, Dr. Lightner takes the women inside themselves to hear the voice of God and see the insights which God gives them! Much on the order of the Christian Base Communities model which swept through the poorest barrios in Central and South America two decades ago, Lightner's methodology of engaging ordinary "salt of the earth" African American women in a wrestling match with the Scripture and the "stuff" of their own lives has produced some exciting results.

Those who read Lightner's work will make some startling discoveries about themselves and their relationship with God. They will learn the importance *of* mentoring and the techniques *for* mentoring African American women who are trying to find their way through the racist-sexist wilderness of male domination and white supremacy; and trying to find their true selves in the process.

Men who give this text an honest hearing will find some of their basic assumptions challenged; and if they are prayerful, they might even find themselves significantly changed. Lightner's work makes a significant contribution to the growing corpus of Christian literature that is "Africentric" in perspective and life-changing in effect.

I am grateful to have had Dr. Lightner as a student. I commend her on this, her first work, and look forward to many, many more.

**Dr. Jeremiah A. Wright, Jr.**
United Theological Seminary
March, 1995

# *THE FOCUS*

The preponderance of women in the seven mainline Black denominations in this country is recognized by most. It is common knowledge that women are the main supporters of Black churches both financially and programmatically, while males traditionally hold leadership positions in the Black church.

Because the Black church has not always considered the Black woman as equal with the Black man in the church, the unique needs of the Black woman - spiritual, cultural, social and physical - have not been seriously addressed by male leadership.

God created women to be *"help meet"* for man.

> *And the LORD God said, It is not good that the man should be alone; I will make him an help meet for him.*                    -- Genesis 2:18

Woman was created to work hand in hand with man in the home, church, community, nation and the world for the edification of mankind. Women, as well as men, must be equipped to fulfill their God-given roles. This equipping should come from the institution she so faithfully serves - the church.

This model-in-ministry-project will create a female mentoring program designed to fill the programmatic gap present in the local church. The aim of the Christian mentoring program is to help the women discover their gifts, talents and abilities, and to utilize them to implement  programs necessary for their own spiritual, social, mental and physical developments as they perceive their needs, rather than depend solely on male leadership in the church to take the initiative to provide adequate women's ministries.

The aim will be to provide a forum for women to come together for the specific purpose of studying the Bible with an emphasis on the female hermeneutic.  These women will learn mentoring techniques and how to utilize them to strengthen and encourage other women.  She will become *"help meet"* in the home, church, community, nation and the world.

This project was designed to implement a female mentoring program at Mount Calvary African Methodist Episcopal Church, Towson, Maryland, by teaching mentoring skills through twelve sessions of Bible study and dialogue.

We utilized the Bible and books authored by African American women, written with a female hermeneutic.  The lessons were designed to encourage women to fully examine the lives of biblical women and to encourage a dialogue about similar contemporary situations.

Results of the model were evaluated by the women's summaries and demonstrated ability to mentor within the group during crisis situations.  The women demonstrated higher levels of self-esteem, self-confidence and leadership capabilities.

# CHAPTER 1

## MEAGER BEGINNINGS

I am a Black woman who has accepted the divine call of God to preach the Word of God. This life changing event occurred in 1981, when my son was 13 years old. I have served as a pastor in the African Methodist Episcopal Church for more than ten years; my son has been one of my strongest supporters.

### TO GOD BE THE GLORY FOR THE GREAT THINGS GOD HAS DONE IN MY LIFE.

I am the youngest of three children born to the late Baxter Roach Farrar and Brooksie Lee Harris Farrar. The cost of hospitalization was too expensive in Raleigh, North Carolina during the late 1940's; therefore, Mrs. Mitchell, the local mid-wife, became the at home "pediatric surgeon" and delivered me as she had my brother, Baxter, before me. My oldest sister, Delores, was born in the local hospital only because of my mother's close encounter with death.

My family was poor, uneducated and unskilled. My parents

separated by the time of my second birthday. I was raised in public housing by three women: my mother, grandmother and great-grandmother. No one in the home had completed high school; yet, these women were the primary positive influences in my life. While they lacked educational knowledge, they over compensated in their knowledge of Christ and Christian ethics. My Christian foundation was solid and I was taught to love and serve God.

## A BRAND NEW WORLD

As a young girl, I grew up in the heart of segregation—"colored" and "white" water fountains; "colored women" and "white ladies" restrooms; carryout only lunches or sodas at Walgreen's Drug Store; separate schools for colored and white children. Raleigh was totally segregated.

In the summer of my sixteenth year, I had the wonderful experience of visiting family in New York. Prior to travelling to New York on a Greyhound Bus, I had never journeyed beyond Pittsboro, North Carolina, located less than 100 miles from Raleigh. This was an exciting and challenging time for me - exciting because I was introduced to a whole new way of living. For the first time in my life, I lived in a home where a man was the head of the household. I was now part of a family that was self-sufficient—no more welfare! I was a wide-eyed tourist for an entire summer. Little did I know that this was the beginning of a whole new life for me. I met and befriended other young people who, surprisingly, were not preoccupied with the issue of racial differences. I had my first pizza, as well as Chinese and Italian food for the very first time. We attended ethnic festivals in Manhattan and, to my great surprise, there were races other than "colored" and "white" in the world.

The challenge came at the end of the summer when it was time for me to go back home to Raleigh. My life had changed so radically in three short months that I felt I could not joyfully return to my family and the segregated south. We had a family conference during which my uncle and aunt, Doug and Gwen Farrar, agreed that I was welcome to finish my high school education in New York while living with them.

My mother was furious! She demanded that I return home immediately. She even traveled to New York to escort me back home. However, I refused to go. I loved my family and I missed them, but this new world I was being exposed to was intoxicating. Hence, I could not turn back! I believed that to have returned to Raleigh would have been moving backward rather than forward in my new life journey. My mind was made up; there was no turning back.

In September of 1960, I enrolled in Eastern District High School where I graduated three years later. My return trips to Raleigh were very brief. I visited during Christmas breaks and summer vacations. I resumed residency in Raleigh, North Carolina upon my marriage to Mr. Bruce Lightner, a native of Raleigh and the son of a prominent mortician who was later elected as Raleigh's first Black Mayor. To this union, our son Lawrence was born. After three years of marriage, which ended in divorce, I again relocated away from my hometown.

As I reflect upon my life's journey to date, I believe it was the years in New York, the different type of family life, the multicultural high school experience, and having worked at Chemical Bank New York Trust Company that influenced the widening of my horizons. There was a new world out there—places to go, sights to see, people to meet, and so much to learn. From this world would emerge a transformed Ann—a woman who would surprise everyone in her hometown; and in the transformation process, even Ann would be surprised.

The subsequent move from Raleigh, North Carolina to Boston, Massachusetts was the turning point for many changes in my life. For it was there, in Boston, that my life was turned completely around, and the real journey began. I went to higher heights educationally and deeper depths spiritually. Despite the fact that my primary influences were not prepared to encourage or equip me to achieve academically, God had prepared people and put them in my path to encourage and help me on this journey toward becoming the Lord's servant.

In 1972, I applied to and was accepted at Boston University's School of Public Communication. I was one of 27 recipients of the Dr. Martin Luther King, Jr. Scholarship Award. I am proud to state that I am one of only three persons who successfully completed this program.

Prior to enrolling at Boston University, I was employed as a secretary for two Harvard University Law professors - Professor Diane Lund and Professor Derick A. Bell, Jr. Professor Bell was, and is, in the forefront of the civil rights movement. He received national attention in 1992 as he resigned his position as Harvard Law School's only tenured Black law professor, challenging the nation's oldest school to tenure a woman. Both professors convinced me that I was "too intelligent" to continue a career as a secretary and "pushed" me into the academic world. Professor Bell, in his publication, *"Race, Racism and American Law,"* makes reference to my achievements. More specifically, Professor Bell highlights my story as a Black divorced woman, raising a child, going back to college and completing a post graduate degree. This reference is included in his nationwide lectures encouraging women to become achievers.

These mentors and many others (i.e., Dr. Geneva Smitherman of Wayne State University; Dr. Samuel Allen of Boston University; the late Bishop Harrison J. and Mrs. Edith Holland Bryant; my pastor, The Reverend (now Bishop) John R. Bryant and his wife Cecelia Williams Bryant (now Reverend); The Reverend Floyd Flake, my assistant pastor; The Reverend Frank Madison Reid, III, my son's godfather; and my dear friends, Reverend Susan Johnson and Dr. Patricia Wright) all of whom the Lord placed in my path during my "formative" years of Christian and educational growth. All of whom encouraged me and helped me on this road to becoming who God intends for me to be.

## HUSH, HUSH, SOMEBODY'S CALLING MY NAME

Although I was raised in the African Methodist Episcopal Zion Church and attended Sunday School regularly until my adult years, my new life in Christ really began in 1973 at Saint Paul African Methodist Episcopal Church in Cambridge, Massachusetts. It was there that I met the Lord in a more personal way. Prior to that experience, I never knew the joy of salvation even though I professed Christianity.

The Lord began preparing me for ministry in the early 70's. I became a Sunday School teacher and attended Bible study and prayer meeting weekly. It was not unusual for me to be involved in some form of church activity four or five times a week. Additionally, I attended three worship services on Sundays. I started attending spiritual retreats and workshops. Before I realized it, my life was totally centered around the church.

My call to preach was inspired through dreams and visions. I actually saw myself preaching before large audiences of people. I could hear my own voice coming through the radio as other preachers were proclaiming God's word. One morning I woke up singing aloud,

> "Tell them even if they don't believe you,
> Tell them, even if they won't receive you,
> Tell them for me.
> Tell them that I love them and
> I've come to let them know."

Dr. William Myers chronicled my "call" story in his book, *"The Irresistible Urge To Preach,"* under the chapter entitled:

*"I Never Wanted to be a Preacher."* As a matter of fact, I never even knew any women preachers during most of my life. I remember listening to the radio as a child in Raleigh, North Carolina, and hearing a woman preacher named "Sister Gary." However, I never personally met her. In fact, I never consciously questioned why all preachers and pastors I knew were male. This practice, much like segregation in Raleigh, was an accepted norm for which I had no need to question nor challenge at that time.

At Saint Paul African Methodist Episcopal Church, however, I learned that God did, in fact, call women into the ministry just as God called men. Here I witnessed many women such as Reverend Mary Watson Stewart, a pastor in the African Methodist Episcopal Church out of Chicago and Reverend Willie Barrow, also of Chicago, preaching the gospel. Even more, I witnessed women going to the altar and confessing to Reverend Bryant that the Lord had called them to preach the gospel. I began to study about biblical prophetesses, i.e., Miriam (Exodus 15:20); Deborah (Judges 4:4); Huldah (II Kings 22:14); Noadiah (Nehemiah 6:14); Anna (Luke 2:36); and the Daughters of Philip (Acts 21:9). The veil had been lifted. The truth was before me although some men may have discriminated against women saying, "God did not call women to preach." The Word of God is clear. God is not a respecter of persons; God uses whom God chooses, and God never makes a mistake.

It seems strange to me now that I was an adult before I ever heard anyone say anything about women preachers, either positive or negative.

I knew about the Virgin Birth, about the Crucifixion and the Resurrection. I understood the meaning of Communion and Baptism. I believed there was a Heaven for the righteous and a hell for the unrighteous. I believed that Jesus was coming back to receive the church. I even knew that Jesus' twelve disciples were males, but I have no recollection of a theology on women preachers ever being taught or preached about in my presence.

Perhaps it never entered my mind because I was not introduced to the feminist movement until the 1970's. I realize now that I was somewhat of a conformist, accepting things for what they were; never challenging, never probing, never "rocking the boat." I never asked about segregated facilities in North Carolina; that's just the way things were! It was really only after entering college that I began to expand my horizons and exercise my abilities to question and to reason and to probe into the status quo, spiritually and socially.

Although church, home and community had provided me with a fundamental understanding of who God was, at Saint Paul I realized that there was much knowledge I still lacked; I was hungry to learn. I always believed that God was real. I prayed every night, even when I was not involved in a church. I believed that God answered prayer, could and did heal sick people and that God would take care of me and my family. I believed that the Sabbath day belonged to the Lord. I did unto others as I would have them do unto me. I knew the Decalogue and was mindful of the laws of God in my daily living. I didn't always keep them, but I asked forgiveness and tried to be obedient to God's word.

## I PUT AWAY CHILDISH THINGS

The proper foundations were always there in my life, but I suppose that just as I see happening in the lives of those I pastor, it does not all come together at the same time for all of us. *"My people are destroyed for lack of knowledge ... "* (Hosea 4:6). I have taken many young girls under my wings for this very reason. They have no idea about what is actually going on around them in the church or at home. I certainly did not as an adolescent, or as a young woman; and many of them have even less support or mentoring than I had. This journey has taught me

7

that "every sister needs a sister."

It was at Saint Paul African Methodist Episcopal Church in Cambridge, Massachusetts, under the ministry of the Reverend John R. Bryant, that I began to study the Word of God and become aware of theological issues such as women in the Church and in ministry, being Christian and Black, the gifts of the Holy Spirit in operation today, and the role of the Church in the community.

At that phase of my spiritual development I became aware that not only did I have little or no knowledge of women in ministry (not just the ordained and pastoral ministry, but various other ministries as well), but also that prior to Saint Paul, I had never been involved in a church that had women serving on the ministerial staff or that had specific ministries for women. These programs were developed by Cecelia Williams Bryant through the Missionary Society at Saint Paul. This exceptionally talented woman developed workshops, seminars and other special gatherings such as women's prayer breakfasts, luncheons and retreats, all designed to enhance the spiritual and cultural growth of the women in the church and community. These events escalated and developed into an international conference for Black women in Baltimore in 1978 called "Behold The Woman," where hundreds of women gathered for a weekend of workshops, exhibits, fellowship and worship.

## WHY WAS I COMPELLED?

It was then that I recognized the void in both my personal life and the church where women ministries or programs of substance were concerned. An old adage that says, "you don't miss what you never had" rings true. Prior to my exposure to these invaluable sessions, I had never missed not having the benefit of ministries geared toward the specific needs of women.

How differently my life might have developed if there had

been women in the church during my adolescent and young adult lifetime; women who would share with me about womanhood, relationships, marriage, child rearing, education and, most of all, my potential as a Black woman in Christ Jesus. I believe my life could have been radically different. I would probably have grown up less insecure and uncertain about what I wanted in life and probably would have had more courage to pursue life's greater opportunities. While the women in my immediate family had my best interest at heart, both spiritually and socially, they lacked the ability to prepare me for educational and career challenges. We can only share that which we have learned or experienced. Surely there were other persons in the church who, if a mentoring program had been initiated, could have filled the gaps my family was not equipped to handle.

This project will show that women are often natural mentors. I believe, however, that women need leadership and encouragement even in the area of mentoring. They must come to understand that they can make a significant difference in the lives of other women and in society in general.

I have come to understand both from my personal and spiritual growth and development and from working with women in the church setting, that women in general know very little about the Bible and its reference to the role of women in the salvational plan of the world. Too many women do not yet know if they were created to be a "curse" or a "blessing." This lack of knowledge left me hungry and thirsty for I knew not what. After exploring the Word of God, however, and seeing God's actions in the lives of women, I began to understand my place in the church and the world more clearly. Dr. Renita Weems apparently experienced the same dilemma. She writes:

> Dutifully, we have sat through sermons, lectures and Bible study lessons nodding when appropriate, copiously taking notes when expected and when called upon, obediently recapitulating what we have been told. All

the while our souls have remained starved for a new revelation on the women in salvation history. Surely God did not mean for us to be a footnote to redemption.[1]

## MINISTRY BIRTHED IN MY PERSONAL LIFE

I have been on this spiritual journey for twenty years and in full-time ministry for twelve years. God has shown me that ministry must continue outside the walls of the church rather than only during the Sunday morning services. Although it can become very taxing—those who would mentor must be available for phone calls and sessions during the week.

God uses me in the pastoral ministry to bring young confused women and girls under my wings and into my home in order that they might draw strength from one who was not so long ago afraid, confused, and hurting herself. My home often becomes a sanctuary for a young woman living with a life threatening disease called cystic fibrosis, a young woman who has grown to trust me with her deepest fears and pains. Two years ago, I encouraged, and paid for, a young man in my parish to take voice lessons to improve and pursue the gift God had given him. That young man, in turn, taught a six-year-old at our church to play the drums for our worship services. They are both a great asset to our music ministry.

Mentoring, or hands-on ministry, is as important to me as preaching a dynamic, life-changing sermon, or presiding over a church conference. This is simply a personal demonstration of how mentoring takes place in our lives when we take the time to see one another's needs and decide to reach out in whatever way we can.

# CHAPTER TWO

## INTRODUCTION TO MODEL

This "model-in-ministry" project demonstrates a women's ministry that will help fill the programmatic gap for women in the local church. Its aim is to train women to develop and implement programs necessary for their own spiritual, social, mental and physical development as they perceive their needs, rather than depending solely on male leaders in the church to take the initiative to provide adequate women's ministries.

This is not to say that males cannot effectively mentor females in the church. My own father in the ministry, Dr. John R. Bryant, is an excellent example of a man's ability to support, teach and encourage women in ministry as well as lay women in the church. Thirteen of the fourteen women pastoring in the Baltimore Conference of the Second Episcopal District of the African Methodist Episcopal Church came out of Bethel African Methodist Episcopal Church in Baltimore, where Dr. Bryant served as pastor for thirteen years. They consider Dr. Bryant their father in the ministry.

In addition to these Baltimore pastors, there are many around the country now serving both as ordained ministers and gifted lay persons, who were also mentored by Dr. Bryant, and are making an impact on the lives of people in their churches.

This project aims to provide ministries that will both nurture Christian women and help them identify and use their gifts and talents to develop programs and to mentor other women. Initially, I purposed to design an "African Rites of Passage Program" for adolescent females in the Black church. However, I later came to the conclusion that I should follow the Titus model (Titus 2:3-4) and first train the women who will in turn be equipped to reach back and mentor the young girls and other women in our churches.

I reached this conclusion after having organized and implemented several programs for our young girls at Mount Calvary. I realized that although the women of the church were willing and eager to assist in these ministries, I was the primary source of leadership. I orchestrated, and everyone obediently followed. However, after the events took place, the young girls totally relied on me to mentor and support them through their various dilemmas.

I realized that even though I was the pastor, I was not the only person capable of mentoring other girls and women in the church. However, the majority of the women obviously did not feel equipped to do all they witnessed their pastor doing with regard to these younger women in the church. It became obvious to me that the women were as hungry for mentoring as were the young girls. Out of their personal need to be a part of the group and to partake in the sessions planned for the young girls, older women were eagerly volunteering to help.

There were also some internal congregational circumstances, which will be discussed in the method section, that prevented the women from bonding and sharing with each other. However, after observing the needs of the young girls and women more closely, I realized that the model in the second chapter of Titus was needed in this situation. The older women must teach the young women. But the older women need guidance and assistance in order to fulfill their biblical role in the church and community.

"Sisters Sharing" is about equipping the women to release the power and the gifts they already possess to the end of mentoring other females.

This model utilized a study group which used both the Bible and various other books in the area of women's studies that discuss the lives of women in the Bible as well as the lives of women today. These resources introduced a new biblical hermeneutic in that they presented biblical women in a positive light while showing, from a modern standpoint, how their lives often mirrored and informed the lives of today's woman. Our main textbook was "*Just A Sister Away*," by Dr. Renita Weems.

This project was designed to breathe life into the Scriptures that model women mentoring women and that describe various women's relationships and lifestyles in biblical times. Examples are Titus 2:3-5, the Book of Ruth, the stories of Jephthah's daughter, Martha and Mary and Sarah and Hagar. These, and other biblical models, were utilized to show the connection that women have always had without regard to age, culture or religion. The project also described other women's support groups that enhanced the lives of women in the local Black church.

In their work, *"The Black Church in the African-American Experience,"* C. Eric Lincoln and Lawrence H. Mamiya write:

> All of the seven mainline Black denominations are characterized by a predominantly female membership and a largely male leadership, despite the fact that the major programs of the Black church in politics, economics, or music depend heavily upon women for their promotion and success.[2]

The African Methodist Episcopal Church, whose dominating population is also women, is ripe as a testing ground for women's ministries. It is interesting to note that the African Methodist Episcopal Church is now producing more women in ministry than men in many of her 19 episcopal districts. For example, in the district where I serve, the Second Episcopal District, Baltimore Conference, there are more than 100 women ministers serving in various local churches.

Being accepted in ministry has been a struggle for women from the beginning of the African Methodist Episcopal Church. This change of status came about during the 1950's and 60's, after centuries of protest and struggle by African Methodist Episcopal women such as Mrs. Jarena Lee, who preached during Bishop Richard Allen's time in the 1800's. After Richard Allen, founder of the African Methodist Episcopal Church in 1787, heard of her call, his response was, "... the Discipline of the African Methodist Episcopal Church knows nothing at all about women who are called."[3]

Mrs. Jarena Lee was never ordained and never held a position of leadership in the African Methodist Episcopal Church. Jarena Lee's response to Allen and the African Methodist Episcopal Church was:

> Oh, how careful ought we be, lest through our by-laws of church government and discipline we bring into disrepute even the Word of life. For as unseemly as it may appear nowadays for a woman to preach, it should be remembered that nothing is impossible with God. And why should it be thought impossible, heterodox, or improper for a woman to preach, see the Savior died for the woman as well as the man.[4]

Historically, the pulpit was the only place where the Black male felt powerful, important and in leadership. However, today, women are entering ministry prepared both academically and spiritually to lead God's people toward liberation. The testimony of Mrs. Jarena Lee is evidence of the fact that women ministers, women teachers, women evangelists, women bishops, women congresspersons and women senators did not get to this place of leadership solely on their own merit. Women stand on the shoulders of those who fought for the cause of women, often not living to see the fruit of their labor—women standing in positions denied our foremothers like Mrs. Jarena Lee. Reverend Lillian Frier Webb, president, Connectional Council of Women in Ministry of the African Methodist Episcopal Church, in the preface to *"Religious Experiences and Journal of Mrs. Jarena Lee, A Preach'in Woman,"* writes:

> Black women never had the time to feel oppressed by Black men. They were too busy surviving the evils of racism. However, conflicts did exist in one area when a few dauntless, pioneering women dared to proclaim a "call."[5]

Although there are fourteen women pastors in the Baltimore conference, there are more than 80 other women ministers in this conference who, because of lack of available positions, are not able to hold the office of pastor. Perhaps at a later time someone will research other options for ministries women might pursue. The point here is that God has women in the church who are prepared to teach and preach and to mentor other women.

If male pastors were open to the idea, these women could come into local churches and start women's ministries or teach existing women how to develop ministries that will edify the body of Christ. I am not suggesting that these women are only capable of mentoring other women. I am saying, rather, that these women have training in various fields and could assist both men and women in unlimited ways.

> If the man may preach, because the Saviour died for him, why not the woman? seeing He died for her also. Is he not a whole Saviour, instead of a half one? as those who hold it wrong for a woman to preach, would seem to make

it appear.

> Then that little man in black there, he says women can't
> have as much rights as men, because Christ wasn't a
> woman! Where did your Christ come from? Where did
> your Christ come from? From God and a woman! Man
> had nothing to do with Him.[6]

While this project is not specifically about women in the ordained ministry, it is about women doing ministry, the ministry of mentoring other women. In light of the fact that many women yet feel that there is no place for women in ministry, women must be willing to change their attitudes about a woman's place in the church. This is absolutely necessary because the majority of the women's groups will be led by women, some of whom could be ordained ministers and pastors. There is no question that all too many women have been taught to believe verbatim the text:

> *Let your women keep silence in the churches: for it is*
> *not permitted unto them to speak; but they are com-*
> *manded to be under obedience, as also saith the law.*
> -- I Corinthians 14:34

Too many men and women believe that women ought to be seen in the church and not heard. Of the fourteen women pastoring African Methodist Episcopal churches in the Baltimore Annual Conference, all but one is seminary trained. Many of these women are serving in the less desirable "far and remote places." In spite of the women's preparedness and dedication, word has come from other churches that the people (bear in mind that some 70% of the people are females) do not want a woman pastor.

Mrs. Reba Bass Gilbert, a pastor's wife in Detroit was recently quoted in an article entitled *"Women in the Clergy"* in the *Detroit News* regarding women's acceptance of other women in the ministry. "They haven't found any place in the Bible where it says God called a woman to preach."[7] It is sad to report that this graveyard mentality yet exists in all too many of our churches. Women remain in bondage, a bondage that has been placed on them by the loose interpretation and misinterpretation of Scripture from the Word of God which intends to liberate all of God's people. *"You shall know the truth and the truth shall make you free."* (St. John 8:32)  C. Eric Lincoln and Lawrence H. Mamiya record an incident that supports this contention.

> In the sanctuary of a black Baptist church in Chicago in 1971, at a meeting of the National Committee of Black Churchmen, the following incident took place. Two black women approached the pulpit at different times during the meeting: one was a theology student, so that she could place a recording device; and the other was a Presbyterian church executive who wished to address the committee. The pastor approached each woman and asked her to remove herself from the pulpit area, explaining that the women church officers had passed a ruling that no woman could stand behind the pulpit for any reason. They wanted to ensure that no woman would be elevated over another in the church, and they insisted that the image of the clergy should remain exclusively male. This incident is one illustration of the fact that traditionally in the Black Church, the pulpit has been viewed as "men's space" and the pew as "women's place."[8]

Men and women generally follow their leadership.  Therefore, male clergy persons must begin to take a stand for women preachers if congregations are expected to receive women in the pulpit.  All too often male clergy waiver in their position on women in ministry.  Reverend Gerald Adams, in the *Detroit News* article responds, "The Bible doesn't talk about women preachers, it talks about men and we hold to that tradition.  I don't question God's calling.  I believe God can call whomever He chooses.  But some of the brothers and sisters don't feel that way."[9]

I believe, however, that once women are introduced to a new hermeneutic which shines a positive light on women in the Bible and what their roles and potential can be in today's church and society, women will begin to feel better about themselves and thereby become more accepting of other women in whatever roles they choose to fulfill. Both of the churches to which I have been appointed to serve had never had a female pastor. Many members had never heard a woman preach. But, after serving them, both churches have requested that their next pastor be a woman.

## WHY THE MODEL WAS DEVELOPED

This model-in-ministry was developed as a result of my dissatisfaction with the obvious neglect of God's women in the local church. By neglect I mean that women's needs are not being adequately addressed or met by most congregations' current programming. I have met women from across the country who attest to the fact that local churches across denominational lines are not providing ministries designed to meet the needs of the majority of their congregations, the female. This model was developed to provide an avenue for women to come together for the specific purpose of studying the Bible with an emphasis on the female hermeneutic; sharing dialogue around the issues raised about women in the Bible in modern times; gathering literature by Black women authors that speak to who we are as Black women and Black Christian women; and learning by training in counseling skills how to mentor other females with whom we are in contact. This model will encourage the women in the local church to assess the needs of women in general in the congregation and develop programs that will meet those needs.

This model is needed because the gifts and talents of women are not being fully utilized in leadership positions in the church or to develop programs necessary to empower women to be both the *"help meet"* God created her to be and the mentor she can be. How can we expect young women in the church to aspire to leadership positions when they have no models in the church? Young women will most likely assume, as I did for so many years, that women do not belong in positions of authority, especially the pulpit, and remain "dutiful" pew members.

Most will agree with Drs. Lincoln and Mamiya that "all of the seven mainline Black denominations are characterized by a predominantly female membership and a largely male leadership."[10] Yet, many, if not most, churches do not have ministries geared toward the spiritual, cultural and physical development of its women, nor are women found occupying seats of leadership and authority in the church.

Just as the creation would not have been complete without woman, the church cannot be complete without women. God's intention for women, is stated in Genesis 2:18:

> *"And the Lord God said, it is not good that man should be alone. I will make him an help meet for him."*

The Bible does not suggest that when God created woman she was to be considered less important than the man God created. However, because they have traditionally been misused and abused, women need special nurturing in order to fulfill their roles as "helpers" in the home, church, community, nation and the world. The church can and must be the catalyst for this nurturing process so that women will fully realize God's plan and activity in their total development.

Women need a foundation, either spiritual or otherwise, to be good mentors. A woman can only share what she has learned or experienced. The old adage is true in the case of women being spiritual mentors to other women. "You can't lead where you don't go, and you can't teach what you don't know." The failure of the church has been that she has not provided adequate teachings for the women of God to provide them with tools to become effective spiritual mentors. Have women been deliberately overlooked in the programming of the church? Or, was it simply an oversight on the part of the pastor and church leaders? Perhaps no one thought the women needed training in the Word of God ... that it was sufficient for her to know her way around the church kitchen, usher at the door and sing in the choir. Perhaps it was because it was not thought to be her place to learn the Word of God in more detail. Perhaps church leaders thought, like Jewish males of old, that women should not attend the rabbinical schools (seminaries) or sit with the men while the law (Bible) was being taught.

I do not necessarily think that women have been deliberately deprived of sound teachings in order to keep them ignorant of the liberating Word of God. Even if this were the case, however, women cannot totally blame male leadership. Women are capable of taking responsibility for their own lives and pursuing what they want and need. If women don't allow themselves to become "object" rather than "subject," as Bell Hooks terms taking charge of our lives and situations in her work, *"Talking Back,"* they will have more control over policies that directly affect their life.

## WOMEN MUST "COME TO VOICE"

I contend that women have been left out of the inner workings of the church partly because we have been silent too long about matters that directly concern us. We are cautioned by feminist author, Patricia Hill Collins, in *"Black Feminist Thought"* to come to know ourselves and to develop a strong sense of who we are. Collins says: "self definition is important in resisting oppression. Without this inner knowledge of self, we can never effectively battle the demons of race, sex and class oppression."[11]

In this work, Collins centers her readers around the premise that "all African-American women encounter the common theme of having our work and family experiences shaped by the interlocking nature of race, gender and class oppression."[12]

Women must begin to define the specifics of their needs as members of the body of Christ. A strong Black feminist voice is needed because, as Collins states:

> ... All African-American women share the common experience of being Black women in a society that denigrates women of African descent ... Black women's vulnerability to assaults in the workplace, on the street, and at home has stimulated Black women's independence and self-reliance. In spite of differences created by historical era, age, social class, sexual orientation, or ethnicity, the legacy of struggle against racism and sexism is a common thread bonding African-American Women.[13]

Women must work to assure that ministries are in place that serve to edify this unique part of the congregation. They must learn what the Bible teaches about women, and not allow others to define who they are and what their role is in the body of Christ.

All too often, Black women have been defined by various others, men and women, both Black and White. In the church, just as in the larger society, it is my contention that the Black woman must speak up and speak out for her needs and rights in the church. Too long she has allowed others to be her voice. Author Bell Hooks asserts that we must "come to voice." She cautions the Black feminist to be careful and aware of what she is speaking:

> In celebrating our coming to voice, Third World women, African-American women must work against speaking as "others," speaking to difference as it is constructed in the white-supremacist imagination. It is therefore crucial that

we search our hearts and our words to see if our true aim is liberation, to make sure they do not suppress, trap, or confine ... [and] to know who listens, we must be in dialogue. We must be speaking with and not just speaking to. In hearing responses, we come to understand whether our words act to resist, to transform, to move ...[14]

Another prominent theme of Hooks' is that the Black woman must consciously move from being "object" to becoming "subject." She writes:

The most important of our work—the work of liberation—demands of us that we make a new language, that we create the oppositional discourse, the liberatory voice ... This speech, this liberatory voice, emerges only when the oppressed experience self recovery. Paulo Freire asserts in Pedagogy of the Oppressed, "We cannot enter the struggle as objects in order to later become subjects." The act of becoming subject is yet another way to speak the process of self-recovery.[15]

## WOMAN TO WOMAN

Women mentor out of their own knowledge and experience. Therefore, there are different areas and different levels of mentoring taking place among women.

A woman who is versed in the Bible will be able to both teach and provide encouragement from the Word of God, directing other women to Scriptures that help address their personal problems or circumstances. However, a woman may not know the Bible very well and yet be able to give sound Christian advice based on her faith and experiences in the faith. Other women, who may not be in relationship with the Lord, can still mentor women in whatever area they are familiar, be it educationally, culturally or socially.

Women share out of common experiences - experiences

which ofttimes males cannot relate to simply because they have not had the experience. Common ground binds women together. For example, a woman who is pregnant with her first child will consult another woman for advice and dialogue rather than her husband or male friend. A woman who has undergone a hysterectomy, mastectomy, miscarriage, abortion or some other experience that is limited to the female sex, is likely to seek out other women who have had the same experience for comfort and advice as opposed to a male who often is at a loss for words and adequate support during these trying times in a woman's life. This is not to say that men cannot offer comfort or support. They can and often do. However, I have found that another woman is able to relate on a more personal level than even the most caring man. She can truthfully say, "I know how you feel," or "I understand," and speak existentially.

A young woman at Mount Calvary underwent a mastectomy and was having a difficult time dealing with the new and uncomfortable reality of living with one breast as a single woman. After counseling with her on a spiritual level about the blessing of life itself, I referred her to another woman in the church who has also had a mastectomy performed. This woman had worked through the trauma and was able to provide counselling and encouragement to the younger woman. The younger woman came away feeling much better and realized that life goes on and that there was someone she could share with when she felt depressed. Someone who would understand from experience.

I have talked with many women who have changed from male gynecologists to female gynecologists, saying that a female is more understanding, gentle and willing to share more details about procedures than are males. I personally switched to a female gynecologist over twelve years ago. I, too, find a woman gynecologists much easier to talk with about female problems than a male gynecologist.

Another incident in our church demonstrates how women

mentor women based on their own experiences. A teenage girl was being made to feel badly by the pressures of her teenager peers because she was 18 and had not lost her virginity. She came to me with her concerns and fears about feeling pressured into having sexual relations before she was ready. I introduced her to another young lady whom I had mentored since she was 15 years old, who was also a virgin and had shared similar experiences with me about being teased and pressured by both males and females. Their coming together provided support and friendship for both of these young ladies. They were being mentored probably without even consciously knowing it.

I submit that this is the typical kind of mentoring that goes on between women on a day to day basis. The intent of this project is to encourage churches to provide opportunities for women to study the Word of God on a systematic basis in order that they might be able to share with other women, with whom they naturally come in contact, what God's word says about our particular situations. In addition to her natural ability to support and encourage women, she will be able to use God's word as a foundation for her mentoring.

This project examined Scripture lessons that speak to the woman's life experiences such as the bond developed between Ruth and Naomi; Esther's (Hadassah's) female rights of passage in preparation to become queen and to save the Jewish nation; Sarah and Hagar's tumultuous relationship; Martha and Mary's differing personalities and interests. These, and many other biblical stories relating to the lives of women, helped us to dialogue about how we as Christian women can handle certain situations in our personal lives.

## SISTERS SHARING

There are natural circumstances that bring women together which can result in bonding and mentoring. This was true in biblical times and it is true today.

## Female Waterdrawers:

1. I Samuel 9:11: ... *as they drew near the city, they met young maidens drawing water ...*
2. Exodus 2:16: *Now the priest of Midian had seven daughters: and they came to draw water, and filled the troughs to water their father's flock.*
3. St. John 4:7: ... *there cometh a woman of Samaria to draw water: Jesus saith unto her, give me to drink.*

## Musical Women:

1. I Samuel 18:6-7: ... *and it came to pass as they came, when David was returned from the slaughter of Philistine, that women came out of all cities of Israel, singing and dancing, to meet King Saul, with tabrets, with joy, and with instruments of musick. And the women answered one to another as they played, and said, Saul hath slain his thousands, and David his ten thousands.*
2. Exodus 15:20-21: *And Miriam the prophetess, the sister of Aaron, took a timbrel in her hand; and all the women went out after her with timbrels and with dances. And Miriam answered them, Sing ye to the Lord, for he hath triumphed gloriously; the horse and his rider hath he thrown into the sea.*

## Harems - The House of Women:

Esther 2:8-9: *So it came to pass, when the king's commandment and his decree was heard, and when many maidens were gathered together unto Shushan the palace, to the custody of Hegai, that Esther was brought also unto the king's house, to the custody of Hegai, keeper of the women. And the maiden pleased him; and he speedily gave her things for purification, with such things as belonged to her, and seven maidens, which were meet to be given her, out of the king's house: and he preferred her and her maids unto the best place of the house of women.*

## Wailing Women:

Judges 11:37-40: *And she said unto her father, let this thing be done for me: let me alone two months, that I may go up and down upon the mountains, that I may bewail my virginity, I and my fellows. And he said, go. And he sent her away for two months, and she went with her companions, and bewailed her virginity upon the mountains. And it came to pass at the end of two months, that she returned unto her father, who did with her according to his vow which he had vowed: and she knew no man. And it was a custom in Israel, that the daughters of Israel went yearly to lament the daughter of Jephthah the Gileadite four days in a year.*

## Midwives:

Exodus 1:15-16: *And the king of Egypt spake to the Hebrew midwives, which the name of one was Shiphrah, and the name of the other Puah: and he said, when ye do the office of a midwife to the Hebrew women, and see them upon the stools; if it be a son, then ye shall kill him; but if it be a daughter, then she shall live.*

Whether the women were drawing water, or singing and dancing, waiting in the house of women to hear if they would be called in to the king's chambers, delivering babies, or sharing the grief of another woman because of the thoughtless deeds of others, these were prime opportunities for women to bond and mentor one another.

Herbert Lockyer, author of *"All The Women of the Bible"* comments on the I Samuel 9:11 text by calling the time the women spent drawing water as a "recognized female occupation of those times - and one that afforded occasion for family gossip."[16] I find it quite interesting that a male author would think this a time simply for "gossip." From a female point of view, the hermeneutic is quite different. Perhaps males feel that women are so shallow that their time together is never constructive. A female interpreter might see these as times of both fellowship and mentoring. I contend that these "young maidens" engaged in more than "family gossip." Certainly gossip was not on the mind or heart of midwives, Shiphrah and Puah, while the future of Israel was in their hands. And Jephthah's daughter and the wailing women certainly did not use those two months together to engage in "family gossip."

The tradition of women bonding in work situations has continued down through the years. Women are grouped together because of work situations and because of their place in society. In more modern times, our great-grandmothers gathered to make quilts, can fruits and vegetables, sew the family clothing, work in the tobacco and cotton fields, plant family gardens and to worship together.

South African women are left alone to care for the family for months and years while husbands are away working in other townships. I contend that whether it be in large groups or one-on-one, at work or at play, women tend to be natural mentors to other women.

## Can True Fellowship Happen?

Some would say that a women's mentoring program will not work because women find it difficult to get along. These persons say that women are jealous, envious and often quarrelsome. I agree that some women have problems getting along with other women. There were, in fact, contentious women cited in the Bible (Proverbs 19:13; 21:9). Paul also writes in Philippians 4:2: *"I beseech Euodias, and beseech Syntyche, that they be of the same mind in the Lord."*

Notice that Paul did not stop with stating the problem. He offered a solution for these women who had apparently allowed some disagreement to come between them. *"And I entreat thee also, true yokefellow, help these women which labored with me in the gospel."* (Philippians 4:3) Paul realized, and so do I, that when women are of one mind in the Lord, they can work through difficult situations without loosing respect for one another.

We must remember before casting a shadow on women's mentoring projects, that men also have disagreements and yet manage to work together. The Apostle Paul is a prime example. Paul refused to allow John Mark to travel with him because of a prior disagreement. John Mark had not completed a prior missionary journey with Paul, and as a result, Barnabus split from Paul and took John Mark with him. Males have quarrels too!

This certainly does not suggest that men nor women cannot work together, especially when they know Jesus Christ as Lord of their lives. Relationships can be difficult whether between men or women. Not all arguments and splits are reconcilable, even when persons have the Lord in their lives. We know that Paul and Mark reconciled, but Paul and Barnabus did not. Nor is there any record of Euodias and Syntyche reconciling.

I contend, however, that trust can be built. Through Christian nurturing and fellowship we can learn how to handle our disagreements in love. Prayer groups, worship services, dialogue and women's Bible study groups can serve as an opportune time for women to get to know each other at a deeper level, and thereby come to love and support one another more readily.

## A LOOK AT THE MODEL

*Teach the older women ... then they can train the
younger women.* (Titus 2:3-4, *TLB*)

This model of ministry was developed and implemented in a church with a membership of approximately 300 persons of which 70% are female. The core group consisted of 21 women ranging from age 25 to 70. Other women were invited to share in worship services and workshops related to the project. We chose to keep the initial group small for purposes of intimacy, confidence building and the ability to teach and train which requires more personal interaction. Women from other congregations were invited to join the core group. We were thus comprised of African Methodist Episcopal, Baptist, Christian Community and Pentecostal.

We met once a month on Saturday mornings from 8:00 a.m. until approximately 11:00 a.m. The meetings were held at my home with the exception of two which were hosted by group members and the two church services. The group was named "Sisters Sharing"—"Sisters" because of our common relationship with Jesus Christ and because of our common heritage as African-American women who are "Unshamedly Black and Unapologetically Christian."[17] "Sharing" because that is actually what mentoring is.

The basic format of the meetings was as follows:

A. Refreshments and fellowship
B. Form circle, holding hands, for approximately
one-half hour of prayer and praise. Each woman
vocalized her specific prayer needs and also "placed

in the circle" the needs of women both present and outside the group.

C. The lesson was read aloud and dialogue took place from both the planned and impromptu questions arising from the scheduled lesson.

D. Closing instructions, assignments, prayer and further refreshments and fellowship.

The goal of the group was to organize a group of churched women in order to assess the spiritual and social needs of women in the church community. This knowledge would then allow me to further design programs that nurture and develop strong women who are committed to Christ and to each other. The women would be helped to identify and use their gifts and talents, both God-given and acquired, to mentor other women.

As a result of these sessions, every "sister" would come to know that she has a Christian "sister" who will support, teach and encourage her as she develops as a woman, a sister and a mentor. Once the project was completed, those in the pilot group would not only mentor other women outside the group, but they would continue their studies with this "Sisters Sharing" group.

In implementing this model, I utilized monthly Bible classes, training sessions on counseling techniques, prayer partners, fasting and praying days and various worship services designed specifically for women. Evaluation came through the women's writings on reflections of the lessons, autobiographies entitled "Where Am I Coming From and Where Am I Going?" and a questionnaire. The primary goal was that women would become built up and equipped to become *"help meets"* in their homes, churches, communities and the world.

## AND AIN'T I A WOMAN?

The aim of Christian mentoring for African-American

women is to help discover the woman within themselves. She must learn to become comfortable with her womanhood as well as her ethnicity; and she must become comfortable with her Christianity. We must be careful not to destroy her true self. The African-American woman must become her true self from a biblical basis and not a duplicate of the mentor or any other woman, Black or White. Our goal was to enable each woman to be who God wants her to be, not who the mentor was or who the mentor wanted her to become.

In order for each woman to get in touch with her true feelings about herself, the women were encouraged to write about their personal lives using the question the angel asked Hagar in Genesis 16:8, in the wilderness ... where are you coming from, and where are you going?

> *And He said Hagar, Sarai's maid, whence comest thou?*
> *and whether wilt thou go? And she said, I flee from*
> *the face of my mistress Sarai.*

These autobiographies gave explicit examples of the pain, fears, rejections, needs and desires of the Black women who sit in the pew week after week and often hear very little that lifts and liberates them. They must be freed to become God's women (See Appendix, Page 120).

# CHAPTER THREE

## THEOLOGICAL ROOTS

I don't remember a time in my life that I did not believe in God's existence. From my earliest childhood experiences, I most vividly recall Sunday mornings. On this very special day of the week, my great grandmother, Mamma West, would rise earlier than the rest of the family to start the fire in the wood stove and begin preparing breakfast. The family had our "full bath" the Saturday night before. When we arose on Sunday, we hurriedly washed, dressed and prepared for Sunday School, morning worship and possibly afternoon service at Rush Memorial African Methodist Episcopal Zion Church (now Rush Metropolitan African Methodist Episcopal Zion Church) in Raleigh, North Carolina. We very rarely missed church on Sunday. I sang in the children's choir and always had a part in the annual Easter and Christmas plays.

Most of the children in our Sunday School classes at Rush Memorial learned about Jesus' birth, death and resurrection, and to recite the Lord's Prayer and the Apostle's Creed.

My great-grandmother taught me the principles of Christian stewardship at an early age. We were poor and I very seldom had money of my own. Therefore, on Sunday when I was given my offerings for Sunday School and morning worship, I wanted to keep some of the money for myself. However, Mamma West told me that if I gave it to God's house, God would provide all that I needed. I remember that one Sunday after depositing all of my change in the offering plate, someone gave me money to spend after church. That was proof enough for me that God would give to me if I gave to the church. Perhaps that's why even now, I have no problem bringing my tithes and offerings to the house of the Lord. Not only that, but we always witnessed Mamma West deposit her envelope in the tithing plate even though we knew how little we had at home.

Sunday in Raleigh was clearly the "Lord's Day." We were not allowed to do any work on Sunday. Clothes were ironed and prepared on Saturday so that everything would be ready for Sunday. After services, the teenagers could walk "uptown" to Fayetteville Street, Raleigh's commercial area, and visit the State museums and walk around the Capital grounds. We could not attend movies or partake in any entertainment that involved secular music or dancing. Sunday was a holy day, and most families were found observing it. Religious habits and foundations were being formed even then. I had no consciousness of it, but I was being molded for a life of service to the church.

As stated earlier, at the age of fifteen I relocated to Brooklyn, New York, where I lived with my uncle and aunt and their two daughters until I graduated from high school.

Sunday mornings were different in New York. My family there was Roman Catholic, although my aunt had been reared in the Baptist church. My two cousins attended All Saints Catholic School; we attended the 9:00 a.m. mass on Sunday mornings. Mass was quite different from anything I had ever experienced. All of the "genuflecting" and "Hail Marys" were quite boring to one who had become accustomed to extemporaneous prayers, gospel music, Methodist hymns and fiery preaching.

I even missed the "note choir" singing. This small group of elderly people would sing without benefit of instruments. They would get a rhythm going by patting their feet, and after singing the song through one time using the notes, (do-re-me-fa-so-la-ti-do) they would sing the verse and then moan it.

That, however, was in Raleigh. In Brooklyn, the priest spoke Latin and, therefore, none of us could talk about a "message" on the way home as we had often done in Raleigh. For me, it was more ritualistic, cold and formal than I was accustomed. Aside from that, I could not partake of the Holy Eucharist because I was not Catholic. I had grown accustomed to receiving Communion every first Sunday at Rush Memorial.

Sunday didn't seem like the "Lord's Day" in New York. After mass, we would pack the car and go to the beach or into Manhattan for one of the many ethnic festivals that were being held. After mass, we generally did whatever we wanted.

During that time, my uncle's oldest sister, whom we called Aunt Toolie, would come from her live-in domestic job and spend Friday night at our house. Aunt Toolie was a member of the Bibleway Church in Patterson, New Jersey. She would leave Brooklyn on Saturday afternoon by bus and go to Patterson to worship at Bibleway. I asked if I could go with her one weekend; that experience opened my eyes to an entirely new form of worship called Pentecostalism.

They worshipped in a small storefront church with a wood-burning stove in the sanctuary. A small dining room was located at the rear of the sanctuary. A delicious dinner, including Aunt Toolie's homemade rolls, was served every Sunday after worship.

Worship in Raleigh had been a good and positive experience; but, for the first time in my life, worship was really exciting at Bibleway. Everyone was "Brother" or "Sister" or "Elder;" Aunt Toolie was Sister McKetchen.

Although service at the Methodist church was enjoyable, it

was still traditionally Methodist. There was a method. We strictly followed the traditional order of worship every Sunday even if the Holy Spirit wanted to move in a different way. Mrs. McCullough played the piano and Mrs. Thorpe read the announcements. Even until this day, the same women do the same things at Rush. A few of the older members would say an occasional "Amen!" or "Thank you, Jesus!" A sister would get up to do the "holy dance" every now and then. One of the men would moan the same prayer every week. Most of the celebration came from the pulpit when Reverend Harris would get to the climax of his sermon.

Bibleway was different. Service started not with a procession of the choir, but with spontaneous testifying and singing—songs I had never heard. They had drums and tambourines and wash boards and an old piano. And, not just one older sister danced for the Lord, but it seemed like everybody, young and old, was on his or her feet during most of the service which, unlike the one hour service at Rush Memorial, went on for hours.

It is clear to me now that I was not focusing on what the Bishop was preaching because I remember no theological conflicts entering my mind about what I had learned in the Methodist church. I simply enjoyed being around the members of Bibleway and clapping my hands and stomping my feet to the lively music they made unto the Lord. Until this day, I have always believed that the little storefront church in Patterson, New Jersey awakened in me an enthusiasm for making "a joyful noise unto the Lord." I love to praise the Lord!

I did not know the theology of the Apostolic church. I did not know that they did not ordain women as ministers or elders. I did not notice the subservient role the women played.

Aunt Toolie never approved of my preaching God's word. She never once heard me preach; nor did she ever visit the church I pastored before her death in 1987. I had been preaching for six years at that time. I was hurt because I saw her as a strong spiritual influence in my life; but her disapproval did not deter me.

At age nineteen, I started attending the Friendship Baptist Church in Jamaica, New York. There I was later baptized by immersion. The Baptist church did not recognize my earlier "christening" in the Methodist church. I enjoyed worshipping in the Baptist church more than the Methodist church because of their strong gospel music and gospel preaching. It never bothered me that I was in a church outside the denomination in which I was raised. I was being spiritually fed and that was all that mattered.

## A NEW THEOLOGICAL UNDERSTANDING

I didn't join another Methodist church until 1973, and that was the Saint Paul African Methodist Episcopal Church in Cambridge, Massachusetts. Reverend John R. Bryant, the pastor of Saint Paul, brought me back to African Methodism. Saint Paul was the embodiment of everything my soul was searching for. The spirit of the Lord was truly in that place under Pastor Bryant's leadership. Praise and worship were the rule and not the exception. Reverend Bryant preached and the Word came alive in my heart; I asked the Lord Jesus Christ to forgive me of my sins and to come into my heart and be my personal Lord and Savior. That was the beginning of my "new life" in the church, and more importantly, in Christ Jesus. I gained a new love and appreciation for the Word of God, both preached and written.

The Scriptures took on new meaning. I now owned a personal Bible (not just the huge family Bible in my living room). I now had a new understanding of being "saved." Romans 10:9 says, *"If thou shalt confess with thy mouth the Lord Jesus, and believe in thine heart that God has raised Him from the dead, thou shalt be saved."* Prior to that, I had not been asked if I was saved or if I wanted to receive the Lord as personal Savior.

When I received my first Holy Communion after my salvation was secured, I cried a river of tears. Now I understood Isaiah 53:5, *"... but he was wounded for our transgressions, he was bruised for our iniquities; the chastisement of our peace was upon him and with his stripes we are healed."*

As a child and young adult, I had always thought that the Holy Ghost, or Holy Spirit, was a shout or the holy dance I sometimes saw on Sunday. Whenever someone expressed any emotion—crying out, dancing, or running around the church—someone would say that the person "got the Holy Ghost in church today." To my understanding, Bibleway and Rush Memorial had the Holy Ghost; the Catholic church did not.

At Saint Paul, I learned who the Bible says the Holy Spirit is, and I invited Him to fill me with His power and to lead and control my life. My "upper room experience"[18] happened one Friday night after I had fasted and prayed for three days. There were about 30 other people in the room; some had already received the infilling of the Holy Spirit; others were "tarrying;" some prayed extemporaneous prayers aloud. Others sang:

> Come on down, come on down,
> Lord, let your Holy Ghost come on down.

Soon I was engulfed with a peace and a sense of calm like I had never experienced. At the same time, my whole body began to quiver, and tears—rivers of tears—began to flow from my heart to my eyes. This was my "Pentecost"! Acts 2 came alive for me! I knew without a doubt that the Holy Spirit had come fully into my life. I fell to my knees in praise and thanksgiving even as others around me experienced His presence in various ways. Amid the speaking in tongues, dancing out of control, falling out in a trance; I, and others, laid prostrate before God in praise and thanksgiving.

I am aware that there are Scriptures, such as Acts 19:6, which say that when people were filled with the Holy Spirit they spoke in tongues. *"And when Paul had laid his hands upon them, the Holy Ghost came on them; and they spake with tongues, and prophesied."*

It is interesting that these same denominations, teaching that speaking in tongues is the evidence of the Holy Spirit, prompt women to *speak in tongues*, but they omit the last part of the verse, *"and prophesied."* If women can speak in tongues, why can't women preach the Word of God, which ultimately is what prophesying is? Does not the prophet Joel declare:

> *And it shall come to pass afterward, that I will pour out my spirit upon all flesh; and your sons and your daughters shall prophesy, and your old men shall dream dreams, your young men shall see visions. And also upon the servants and upon the handmaids in those days will I pour out my spirit.*
> -- Joel 2:28-29

I had now been acquainted with five denominations – African Methodist Episcopal Zion, African Methodist Episcopal, Roman Catholic, Apostolic and Baptist. I had not seen women in ministry or strong leadership positions until I joined Saint Paul. It was always the men who were up front—speaking from the pulpit (except in Sunday School) serving on the deacon, steward and trustee boards. Even the acolytes in the Roman Catholic church were male. I began to wonder why it was that the majority of worshippers in all of these churches were female, but the males were always in the positions of leadership.

I heard preaching and teaching on the Apostle Paul's view of women in the church: *"and if they will learn any thing, let them ask their husbands at home: for it is a shame for women to speak in the church"* (I Corinthians 14:35). *"But every woman that prayeth or prophesieth with her head uncovered dishonoureth her head: for that is even all one as if she were shaven"* (I Corinthians 11:5).

The preponderance of women in the majority of our local churches indicates that women have been steadfast in their commitment to the church and that they love the Lord in spite of the hardships they face in the church. This project revealed that women's needs (spiritual, social and cultural) are not being met in far too many local churches.

I have observed in churches I frequent, that many, if not most, do not have any ongoing women's ministries in operation. Much of this may have to do with the fact that since Judaism, women have been regarded as second class citizens, or inferior to males, in the church and society. Aida Besancon Spencer, writes the following in her work, *"Beyond The Curse"*:

> Many persons have referred to the Jewish daily prayer as proof of the low view of women in all Jewish eyes:
> *Blessed is He who did not make me a Gentile;*
> *Blessed is He who did not make me a woman;*
> *Blessed is He who did not make me an*
> *uneducated man (or a slave).*
> (Tosephta 7:16-18 on t. Ber. 13b or b. Menah 43b).[19]

The woman's seating in the Jewish temple was indicative of this discrimination. The woman's court was located in the rear of the temple (separated from her family members) just ahead of the Gentile court. The men were seated in the men's court located at the front of the temple. Women were not allowed to study the Torah, the law, or join discussions on matters of the law. Women were not allowed to converse with their husbands, or men in general, in public; it was woman's primary duty to bear children, preferably male children, for her husband.

Many modern churches' theology still embraces Old Testament customs such as covering of the head, silencing of women, and forbidding women to teach, preach or hold certain offices (deacons, trustees or pastor). While the above views of women in the Christian church come primarily from a distortion of Paul's writings, responsible biblical scholarship shows that Paul was actually not against women ministers and was speaking from a cultural, not a theological standpoint. Dr. Renita Weems and Dr. Jacqueline Grant write on the issue of whether women should cover their heads in worship (I Corinthians 11:4-7). Dr. Weems writes the following in an article entitled, *"We Have No Such Custom: To Cover or Not To Cover A Woman's Head."*

> The women of Corinth were neither malcontents nor reprobates. They were women with their own interpretations of the traditions handed to them (11:2). Evidently the women had taken seriously and had found liberatory the idea that they were new creations in Christ, made in the image of God, they surely experienced as shame anything that obstructed, obscured, or denied this reality ... To defend wearing veils Paul embarked upon a specious, obscure, and highly suspect argument about honor, glory, and angels and nature. It seems apparent that his feelings on the subject were not so much theological as they were based on custom and the desire to preserve the status quo. Paul first defends veil wearing on the basis of shame and honor. But we do not live in a culture where a woman's hair and its adornments are seen as enticing. A woman does not disgrace herself in our culture by cutting her hair, shaving her head, nor by leaving her head uncovered ...[20]

Even the Apostle Paul, from whose writings most who hold these antiquated views of theology like to quote, wrote in Galatians 3:28: *"There is neither Jew nor Greek, there is neither slave nor free man, there is neither male nor female, for you are all one in Christ Jesus."*

Paul's ministry, in fact, included and accepted women as demonstrated in the sixteenth chapter of Romans:

> *I commend unto you Phoebe our sister, which is a servant of the church which is at Cenchrea: That ye receive her in the Lord as becometh saints, and that ye assist her in whatsoever business she hath need of you: for she hath been a succourer of many, and of myself also.*    -- Romans 16:1-2

> *Greet Priscilla and Aquila, my helpers in Christ Jesus, who*

**41**

*have for my life laid down their own necks; unto whom not only I give thanks, but also all the churches of the Gentiles. Likewise greet the church that is in their house. Salute my well beloved Epae'etus who is the firstfruits of Achaia unto Christ.* -- Romans 16:3-4

*Greet Mary, who bestowed much labor on us.* -- Romans 16:6

*Salute Andronicus and Junia, my kinsmen, and my fellowprisoners, who are of note among the apostles, who also were in Christ before me.* -- Romans 16:7

*Salute Tryphena and Tryphosa, who labored in the Lord. Salute the beloved Persis, which labored much in the Lord.* -- Romans 16:12

These women are noted as co-workers with the Apostle Paul.

More importantly, these churches and denominations that denigrate women refuse to embrace the liberating theology of Jesus Christ Himself who was no respecter of persons. Throughout New Testament Scripture, Jesus related to women in an unorthodox manner—letting all know that He loved and respected women just as He loved and respected men.

His public conversation with the Samaritan woman at the well, St. John 4:5-29, was unacceptable in orthodox Jewish settings; for men did not speak with women in public. Jesus allowed the woman with the issue of blood to touch Him in St. Mark 5:25-34 (See Leviticus 15:25). He allowed Mary to sit at His feet (symbolizing teaching) at Lazarus' home in St. Luke 10:38-42. He forgave the woman caught in the act of adultery in St. John 8:3-11. In spite of the fact that Jews did not regard the word of a woman as "good," Jesus announced His resurrection to a woman, possibly a reformed harlot, and told her to go and tell this good news to His disciples (Matthew 28:10; Mark 16:9; Luke 24:10; John 20:14).

Jesus' behavior with women was not considered acceptable in traditional Jewish settings. His ministry to women demonstrated equal treatment of males and females without regard to customs or traditions.

## "HELP MEET" OR SILENT PARTNER IN THE CHURCH

> *And Adam gave names to all cattle, and to the foul of the air and to every beast of the field; but for Adam there was not found an help meet for him ... And Adam said, This is now bone of my bones, and flesh of my flesh; she shall be called woman, because she was taken out of man.* -- Genesis 2:20,23

My theological foundation is rooted and grounded in the church. From my childhood up to the present, my life has been centered in the church. The community and the home in which I was raised believed in God; there has never been a time in my life when I did not believe in God's existence and power. My family attended church regularly and I was taught to fear and to serve God. The church has been and remains an intricate part of my life. Spiritually, "... it is the mystery of a human-divine institution in which man can find light, pardon and grace for the praise of God's glory."[21]

The church is the called out people of God. The church represents a community of believers in the saving and restoring power of the Lord Jesus Christ. The church is Jesus' bride whom He will return to receive unto Himself. Jesus loves the church; all of her members, both male and female, are important to Him. The church is neither *Jew nor Greek, male nor female.* I contend that the female in the church is as precious in God's sight as is the male. He wants the body to be one member:

> *For as the body is one, and hath many members, and all the members of that one body, being many, are one body so also is Christ.* -- I Corinthians 12:12

The church's one foundation
Is Jesus Christ her Lord;
She is His new creation

43

By water and the Word;
From Heav'n He came and sought her
To be His holy bride;
With His own blood He bought her,
And for her life he died.[22]

## BLACK WOMEN'S RELATIONSHIPS
## WITH ONE ANOTHER

I chose to research and develop a mentoring program for African-American females in the Christian church. This project flowed from my dissatisfaction with the lack of formal training, or mentoring, that our young girls and women are afforded in the church, an institution that should have a strong impact on our lives spiritually, culturally and socially. Collins writes:

> Black women's efforts to find a voice have occurred in at least three safe spaces. One location involves Black women's relationships with one another. In some cases, such as friendships and family interactions, these relationships are informal, private dealings among individuals. In others, as was the case during slavery (D. White 1985), in Black churches (Gilkes 1985), or in Black women's organizations (Gilkes 1982; Giddings 1988), more formal organizational ties have nurtured powerful Black women's communities. As mothers, daughters, sisters and friends to one another, African-American women affirm one another (Myers 1980).[23]

Mentoring is beneficial to the positive development of the African-American female. African-American females are unique; they often bear an undue burden in our society. This has been the case since they were brought to these foreign shores from the Motherland—Africa. Collins agrees:

> All African-Americans share the common experience of being Black women in a society that denigrates women of African descent. This

44

> commonality of experience suggests that certain characteristic
> themes will be prominent in a Black woman's standpoint.[24]

She constantly bears the burden of racism as well as sexism. Her self-esteem is apt to be lower than her white sisters because the society in which she lives does not value her beauty, abilities or her potential. She must be nurtured in order to fulfill her God-given role as a *"... help meet for him."* (Genesis 2:20)

African-American women must affirm one another if they are to develop to their fullest potential. Although Black women can and do have invaluable relationships with women of other cultures, African-American women must be the primary mentors of other African-American women. The old adage "it takes one to know one" is appropriate in this instance. Collins agrees:

> The mother/daughter relationship is one fundamental relationship among Black women. Countless Black mothers have empowered their daughters by passing on the everyday knowledge essential to survival as African-American women ...
>
> In the comfort of daily conversations, through serious conversation and humor, African-American women as sisters and friends affirm one another's humanity, specialness, and right to exist. Black women's fiction such as Toni Cade Bambara's short story The Johnson Girls (1981) and Toni Morrison's novels Sula (1974), The Bluest Eye (1970), and Beloved (1987), is the primary location where Black women's friendships are taken seriously.[25]

Many conversations that take place between Black women are unspoken and unwritten—they are simply felt. One must "walk a mile in her shoes" before one can truly understand and speak experientially. Black women defy the standard definitions of womanhood, thus Sojourner Truth's proverbial question, *"Ain't I a Woman?"*

It takes a Black woman to understand a Black woman. They are sisters by ethnicity—they are all connected to their motherland, Africa, and have many "roots" or "traditions" as well as "struggles" that are common to all African-American women.

The African-American woman's nurturing must also come from the church—from her pastor. The Bible admonishes church leaders to nurture all the people of God.

> *Take heed, therefore unto yourselves, and to all the flock, over which the Holy Ghost hath made you overseers, to feed the church of God, which he hath purchased with his own blood.* -- Acts 20:28

A casual glance at our churches will, I believe, reveal the fact that there is a dire need for such mentoring. Most will agree that Black women make up the larger population of our churches. Collins writes:

> Evelyn Brooks (1983) and Jacqueline Grant (1982) identify the church as one key institution whose centrality to Black community development may have come at the expense of many of the African-American women who constitute the bulk of its membership. Grant asserts, "it is often said that women are the 'backbone' of the church." On the surface, this may appear to be a compliment ... It has become apparent to me that most of the ministers who use this term are referring to location rather than function. What they really mean is that women are in the 'background' and should be kept there.[26]

Too many African-American women are lacking in spiritual and cultural awareness as well as social maturity, and are experiencing the same pitfalls that African-American women outside the church are encountering. There is a lack of knowledge of the Word of God and of our African-Heritage. And as a result, teen-age pregnancy, school dropouts, low self-esteem, lack of purpose and direction, and lack of morals are as prevalent among church going African-American females as they are among the unchurched females. Black women must develop physically, culturally, emotionally, intellectually and spiritually to become whole and complete women. They need responsible guidance and proper models from the African-American community in order to succeed. Mary C. Lewis writes:

> Throughout adolescence, Black females are struggling to define their cultural selves. This is basically a social, emotional and psychological struggle. Thus, a Black female adolescent is seeking to understand what place her Blackness holds in her life, in her view of herself, how she feels about that view, and in what ways society influences her self-image.[27]

The church has been remiss in her responsibility to minister to the "total woman." For while the church has received and presented salvation unto her, the church has not ministered to her total needs. She needs to be saved from sin, yes, but she also needs to be delivered from inbred low self-esteem. She needs salvation, yes, but she also needs both men and women to lead her through a process of becoming an African-American woman by the teaching of the Word of God from an Afrocentric perspective. For, while nature will grow her body and develop her physically *("... and the maid was fair and beautiful ..."* - Esther 2:7), only God can positively develop her mind and her will *("... I also and my maidens will fast likewise"* - Esther 4:16). The church must minister to the whole woman!

Biblical research reveals that women, no matter what their culture, need positive mentors. The book of Ruth demonstrates how the older woman can guide and instruct young women into:

## 1. Positive Self Lifestyles

> *And she said, I pray you, let me glean and gather after the reapers among the sheaves; so she came,*

47

*and hath continued even from the morning until now,
that she tarried a little in the house.*     -- Ruth 2:7

## 2. Cultural Awareness

*And Ruth said, Entreat me not to leave thee, or to
return from following after thee: for whither thou
goest, I will go; and where thou lodgest, I will lodge:
thy people shall be my people, and thy God my God.*
         -- Ruth 1:16

*And Ruth the Moabitess said, He said unto me also,
Thou shalt keep fast by my young men, until they
have ended all my harvest. And Naomi said unto
Ruth her daughter-in-law, It is good, my daughter,
that thou go out with his maidens, that they meet
thee not in any other field. So she kept fast by the
maidens of Boaz to glean unto the end of barley
harvest and of wheat harvest; and dwelt with her
mother-in-law.*          -- Ruth 2:21-23

## 3. Prepare Themselves for Marriage

*Then Naomi her mother-in-law said unto her, My
daughter, shall I not seek rest for thee, that it may
be well with thee? And now is not Boaz of our kin-
dred, with those maidens thou wast? Behold, he
winnoweth barley tonight in the threshing floor.
Wash thyself therefore, and anoint thee, and put thy
raiment upon thee, and get thee down to the floor
but make not thyself known unto the man, until he
shall have done eating and drinking. And it shall
be, when he lieth down, that thou shalt go in, and
uncover his feet, and lay thee down; and he will tell*

*thee what thou shalt do. And she went down into the floor, and did according to all that her mother-in-law bade her. And when Boaz had eaten and drunk, and his heart was merry, he went to lie down at the end of the heap of corn and she came softly, and uncovered his feet, and laid her down. And it came to pass at midnight, that the man was afraid, and turned himself and, behold, a woman lay at his feet. And he said, Who are thou? And she answered, I am Ruth thine handmaid: spread therefore thy skirt over thine handmaid; for thou art a near kinsman. And he said, Blessed be thou of the Lord, my daughter for thou hast shown more kindness in the latter end than at the beginning, inasmuch as thou followest not young men, whether poor or rich. And now, my daughter, fear not; I will do to thee all that thou requirest for all the city of my people doth know that thou art a virtuous woman. And now it is true that I am thy near kinsman howbeit there is a kinsman nearer than I. Tarry this night, and it shall be in the morning, that if he will perform unto thee the part of a kinsman, well; let him do the kinsman's part: but if he will not do the part of a kinsman to thee, then will I do the part of a kinsman to thee, as the Lord liveth lie down until the morning.*

-- Ruth 3:1-13

This principle is also prescribed in New Testament Scripture recorded in Titus 2:1-5:

*But speak thou the things which become sound doctrine: That the aged men be sober, grave, temperate, sound in faith, in charity, in patience. The aged women likewise, that they be in behavior as becometh holiness, not false accusers, not given to much wine, teachers of good things; that they may teach*

**49**

*the young women to be sober, to love their husbands, to love
their children, to be discreet, chaste, keepers at home, good,
obedient to their own husbands, that the word of God be not
blasphemed.*

Older women are to teach or mentor younger women in
proper scriptural, social and cultural behavior. Women must be
mentored so that they, like Naomi, can reach back and give positive advice and direction to the younger women. If this is not
done ... or worse than that, if younger women witness a negative, unholy lifestyle in the adults they see and interact with on a
day to day basis ... the young women will often go astray.

The results are seen in multiple teenage pregnancies and
abortions, school dropouts, welfare dependency, as well as drug
abuse. I have watched it happen time and time again in the
community I serve. I am all the more convinced that the Word
of God is right when it says, *"the aged women likewise, that
they be in behavior as becometh holiness ..."* (Titus 2:3).

The young women in the community have witnessed the
"unholy" life styles of many of the older women and have followed their example. Many of the young women are the prod-
uct of teenage mothers. They have not had the benefit of a "traditional" family lifestyle where mother and father are married
and are raising the children together. They interact on a day to
day basis with women who are school dropouts, welfare recipients and drug abusers.

I am not saying that all of the above is "unholy" or "sinful,"
but it certainly sets a poor example for young women who witness their lifestyles. The African-American community needs
more women who will exhibit *"behavior as becometh holiness."*

The book of Esther unfolds again the need for preparation
and guidance in the life of women who will be God's instruments in our various places in society and church. In the book
of Esther, we see a woman being groomed for an adult role
using components necessary for womanhood. Herein, we find

that men can, and should, be a part of the female's mentoring process.

> *So it came to pass, when the King's commandment and his decree was heard, and when many maidens were gathered together unto Sushan the palace, to the custody of Hegai, that Esther was brought also unto the king's house, to the custody of Hegai, keeper of the women. And the maiden pleased him, and she obtained kindness of him; and he speedily gave her things for purification, with such things as belonged to her, and seven maidens, which were meet to be given her, out of the king's house and he preferred her and her maids unto the best place of the house of the woman.*
> -- Esther 2:8-9

## A PLACE OF PREPARATION

I contend, based on my own personal experiences of being raised in the Christian church, that African-American girls are not receiving adequate preparation for positive lifestyles and for becoming builders of our community both spiritually and culturally. It is appalling to me that never in my childhood or adult experiences in the church, until I joined Saint Paul African Methodist Episcopal Church, did the church hold classes or seminars for young girls or women to talk about who we are in God's church and God's plan.

The churches I attended did not address the special needs and concerns of young girls and women until I encountered Cecelia Williams Bryant and the Missionary Society of Saint Paul. It was then that I was exposed to what is now called "Women's Ministries" which consist of workshops, seminars, luncheons, overnight retreats, rap sessions, and women's Bible studies. In 1978, she organized "Behold The Woman," an international ecumenical conference developed to teach women the art of spiritual discipline. In her work, *Kiamsha*, (Swahili for "that which AWAKEN'S ME") Reverend Williams Bryant pro-

51

duces a spiritual discipline for African-American women.

Women make up the vast majority in most of our Christian churches. The question then becomes, if woman was created to be "helpers" for man, why are there not more programs that speak directly to the needs of these women, both young and old? The answer could lie in the fact that the majority of our Christian churches are headed by males who may not be sensitive to the special needs of females in their congregations.

The need is greater today with more girls growing up in broken homes, drug infested homes, foster homes, abusive homes and homes where the adults are unchurched and untrained academically. Statistics show a continuing rise in teenage pregnancy, drug abusers and school dropouts, even among Christian females. These young females need guidance and support. They need positive Christian role models, both male and female, to help guide them into womanhood. If the church is to mold lives for Christ, she must pay special attention to this unique part of the congregation, the young Black female.

All too often the needs of women, which can be quite different from those of their male counterparts, in our churches are grossly overlooked. I do not believe this to be God's will. Black adolescent females defy simplification. They need and deserve special mentors to help guide them through this difficult period of development. I do not believe that God is pleased that women are not being properly trained to live positive, productive Christian lives.

Woman was created for a purpose, a purpose that neither man nor beast could fill. The church of God cannot afford to overlook the female population in her midst. Rather, the church must purpose to assist in the development process of women who were created to be the *"help meet"* for men.

> *And the Lord God said, It is not good that the man should be alone; I will make him an help meet for him.* -- Genesis 2:18

If she is to accomplish this, she must receive preparation and instruction. This instruction must prepare her to be a "help" in the areas of home, church, community, nation and the world. The church already has the people resources for this preparation and instruction. In her membership can be found people from all walks of life. We must simply use what God has already given us to mentor our young Black females.

My particular interest is spiritual, social and cultural development of African-American females. It is my contention that this group of women desperately needs this mentoring process, perhaps even more than the European female. For the African-American female has the issue of racial discrimination as well as the myriad of other discriminations with which all women in this society must contend. However, as in the case of Esther (Hadassah), although the Black female is viewed as the least likely to succeed, when given a chance she will rise to the top.

> And the king loved Esther above all the women, and she obtained grace and favor in his sight more than all the virgins; so that he set the royal crown upon her head, and made her queen instead of Vashti. -- Esther 2:17

Esther, like today's young Black female, had several obstacles to being chosen as queen:

1. She was a foreigner and did not know the customs well.
2. She came from an oppressed people.
3. She was struggling for her survival as well as the survival of her people.

Esther was indeed, like most Black women, the least likely to succeed, yet she rose to the top.

Dr. Renita Weems, in her work, *"Just A Sister Away,"* discusses the story of Hagar, an Egyptian slave girl, as she flees from Sarai her mistress, in a chapter entitled *"A Mistress, A*

*Maid, and No Mercy."*

> Upon finding Hagar at a spring in the wilderness (Genesis
> 16:7), And the angel of the Lord asked the runaway slave
> the unavoidable question *"Hagar, maid of Sarai, where
> have you come from; and where are you going?"* (Genesis
> 16:8). Hagar was not only broken, she was empty as well,
> too empty to seize her future. From whence she had come,
> she was all too aware *"I am fleeing from my mistress ..."*
> *(Genesis 16:8).* But where she was headed, unfortunately,
> Hagar could not answer.[28]

The angel's question to Hagar, "where have you come from and
where are you going?" is the question for which the church must
help African-American females find answers. Dr. Weems,
throughout this important work, stresses the importance of Black
women bonding together to strengthen and support one another
as we answer the probing question of the angel in Genesis 16:8.

The African-American female must be nurtured by other
women in the African-American tradition - women who know
and serve God; women who have survived slavery in America;
women who have survived abuse (sexual and mental), racism
and sexism; women who have been denied equal rights to education and jobs; women who know and love the African tradition and history; women who can be positive mentors to other
women who must now come through the "coals of fire" that
have been conquered by our foremothers on these foreign shores;
women who have beat the odds; women who refused, and yet
refuse to be relegated to a kitchen or bedroom or nursery;
women like the woman Langston Hughes describes in his poem
*"Mother to Son"*:

> ". . . life for me ain't been no crystal stair."[29]

# CHAPTER FOUR

## THE METHOD

The United Theological Seminary Doctor of Ministry Project mandates that there be participation of the context associates with the candidate. These persons in the local context are referred to as context associates. The purpose of this mandate is to allow persons in the local church, Mount Calvary in this instance, the opportunity to assist the leader in the planning, development, implementation and evaluation of the project.

This project was taught by the pastor of the church who happens to be a female minister. However, the leader does not have to be a pastor or an ordained minister. My experience has shown that a male cannot effectively lead a group of African-American women in a project of this nature. Therefore, if the pastor of the church where this model is to be duplicated happens to be a male, he would do well to search his ministerial staff and congregation for a female who has a heart for God's women, and train these persons to lead the "Sisters Sharing" sessions.

The context associates were four women (ages ranging from 25 to 70) who had been a part of the earlier "Sisters Sharing" group involving the young females in the church two years prior to the formation of this model. Two are life long members of Mount Calvary, and two are more recent members of the church family—one approximately fifteen years and the other only three years. Three of these women are natives of Towson and one is a native of South Carolina who now resides in Baltimore City.

The associates were apprised of the goals and objectives of the project and the time frame under which we were to work. The associates helped gather information on the history of the church and the Towson community. Together we established the most convenient meeting time, and the associates sent monthly meeting reminders, kept track of attendance and provided telephone follow-up to ensure maximum participation. They also handled the refreshments and clean-up following each meeting.

Although the name "Sisters Sharing" was previously used with the younger sisters, it was agreed by the context associates that the name should remain the same as it best fits our project and goals. Webster's Third New International Dictionary defines for us the word "sister" and its derivatives:

> **sister** - a female human being related to another person having the same parent; a female member of a Christian church, often used with a surname or given name; a woman related or linked to another by a common tie or interest; a female human being sharing a common national or racial origin with another.

> **sisterhood** - a community or society of sisters; the state of being a sister.[34]

I selected the title "Sisters Sharing" because of the intimacy I perceive in the word "sister." It suggests union, endearment, culture and sorority. It suggests a road map intergenerationally, for living life to life, and woman to woman; thus we are "Sisters Sharing."

Black women in the church are naturally bonded in at least three areas:

> 1. **Sisters by Ethnicity** - We are all connected to our motherland, Africa and have many "roots" or "traditions" as well as struggles that are common to all African-American women.
>
> 2. **Sisters by Gender** - We are all female. Our gender makes us alike in multitudes of ways which bring about a commonality.
>
> 3. **Sisters in Christ** - We all have a common love for the Lord Jesus Christ.

These three elements give us enough common ground that we should be able to love one another, support one another and share our lives with one another. We do not intend to use the term loosely.

The sessions were announced through our weekly bulletins. Any woman (eighteen and above) was invited to share in this twelve month journey of learning about who we are as African-American Christian women by studying the Word of God and various books by women authors that interpret the biblical passages on women. The women of Mt. Calvary were asked to invite family, friends and co-workers outside our context. Interested persons were to contact the designated context associate.

We agreed to meet once a month, on the first Saturday, from 8:00 a.m., until approximately 11:00 a.m. This early morning meeting would allow the women ample time to perform their regular Saturday activities following our sessions. There were two occasions where I had preaching engagements on our scheduled meeting dates. On one occasion—a prayer luncheon for a woman's group—the women accompanied me. Other times we changed our meeting date to accommodate the leaders' schedule. The women expressed that they did not want a substitute to fill in, and that where needed, we would adjust our schedule to insure the leaders' participation. In addition, while the women wanted to meet on a bi-monthly basis, the leaders' schedule would not permit. Some of the women brought their young children to the sessions. We, therefore, needed to provide entertainment for these toddlers. The children would sometimes watch "Barney" on television, or the parents would bring the childrens' videos or games to provide needed entertainment.

To promote fellowship among the women, the context associates prepared a "Sisters Sharing Directory" listing names, addresses, telephone numbers, birthdates, marital status and parental status of each woman.

While the "Sisters Sharing" directory lists twenty-three women who were regular attendees, the women often brought other women to various "Sisters Sharing" sessions. These women are members of various churches and denominations. Twelve of the regular participants are members of Mount Calvary. Nancy Victor of New Jersey, traveled to Maryland monthly to share in these sessions with her daughter, Tracy Victor, who is a member of Mount Calvary. During this project, one sister who was searching for a new church home joined the Mount Calvary Church family.

The context associates were a tremendous asset to the leader and the project. They handled the administrative details competently and with little need for assistance from the leader. They worked well together despite their differences in age and educational background. Their excitement and enthusiasm quickly spread throughout the group. Future models are cautioned to also select context associates who are both capable and cheerful. It is important that the women demonstrate a friendly attitude with all of the women entering the group. "One sour grape can spoil the bunch."

## The Method

As stated in Chapter 2, *"Introduction to Model,"* our sessions took on a specific format. The following details on the format may be helpful to future groups.

### Refreshments and Fellowship

This segment had a two-fold purpose;

1. We met early, 8:00 a.m.; consequently many of the women had not had their first cup of coffee or tea before leaving home. Light refreshments were needed for both nourishment and stimulation.

2. This was the "ice breaker," a getting to know you period. Especially in the beginning of our sessions, the women did not all know one another and needed opportunities, before the lesson, to get to know one another on a first name basis.

Every woman knew at least one other woman (the person who invited her) and so the tensions were eased in a very short while. I always wore very casual, comfortable clothing, mostly slacks, and encouraged the women to come dressed as comfortably as they wished. I did not wish to be seen as the "pastor," the "heavy," or the formal "church body" of the group. I wanted the women to view me as a "sister" who was interested in helping them learn about themselves from the Word of God and other literature and how to become supporters and mentors to other women. When the women began calling me "Reverend Ann," I felt we had begun to bond and to move toward healing so that we might become healers.

## Prayer Circle

A circle represents a whole, completeness and unity. No matter how many women were in the room, at each session we formed a circle and held hands.

1. I began by welcoming everyone back to our group and praised God for keeping us safe while we were apart. Following the greeting, one of the sisters or I would begin to sing a familiar praise song and the others immediately joined us in praise and worship.

2. I would then invite the women to "place their prayer requests in the circle." The circle was our symbol of unity. We went around the complete circle giving each woman the opportunity to share whatever was on her heart for prayer for herself (her unexpressed pain, her undefined pain) her family, her husband, her friends, her job concerns, her spiritual needs and especially another woman whom she knew was in need of prayer. After each woman voiced her prayer concern, we collectively placed our right foot in the circle (symbolizing our releasing the concern to God) and said in unison, "in the name of Jesus," to signify that we believed God with her for an answer to her prayer. After each woman had an opportunity to speak, I prayed an extemporaneous prayer on behalf of all assembled.

3. The women then took a seat, some on the floor, others on couches or chairs, always in as close a circle format as possible. The women brought refreshments into the living room which also made them feel comfortable and at ease.

4. A review of the last session was given by a volunteer. Some women may have missed the last session and this helped them to catch up as well as to refresh others with where we were in the lessons. Each woman was given an outline of the lesson of the day. The leader then introduced the new lesson. We proceeded with teaching and dialogue until our time was up.

## Closing

At the close of each session, the leader gave remarks and instructions for the next session. Also, the women were given the leaders' preaching schedule so they might attend when possible. We collected $5.00 per month dues for mailings, cards and the upcoming "Sisters Sharing" worship service. The circle now forms again with the women holding hands. The leader or designated person would give the closing prayer. We were instructed to hug each other and give each woman a final word of encouragement.

> Note: As time allowed, the women were encouraged to speak out, and to voice their feelings and opinions. This was very important because all too many women have been silenced in the church, home and in the workplace. Speaking out can be both liberating and healing. Women must be given an opportunity to "come to voice." The value of this will be seen in our discussion on "where are you coming from and where are you going" (Genesis 16:8). It is important for women to speak in the presence of others who are intently listening.

## Resources

"Sisters Sharing" is comprised of women of African descent. I, therefore, wanted to use materials that reflect our Afrocentric heritage. I chose *"Just A Sister Away,"* by Renita J. Weems, as our main textbook. This work is written by a Black woman who felt the need for Black women to have a view of women in the Bible other than the traditional Eurocentric interpretations. Dr. Weems writes in her forword:

> Dutifully, we have sat through sermons, lectures, and Bible study lessons, nodding when appropriate, copiously taking notes when expected and, when called upon, obediently recapitulating what we have been told. All the while our souls have remained starved for a new revelation on the

role of women in salvation history. Surely God did not
mean for us to be a footnote to redemption.[35]

Dr. Weems' intention is: "... to explore the unchartered territory of stories that could give us clues as to what biblical women felt about their lives.[36]

"Just A Sister Away" provided for the "Sisters Sharing" group a feminist hermeneutic with an Afrocentric tone. The Black woman's unique experience cannot be denied in the study of the Bible.

In addition to our regular Saturday sessions, the women participated in the following worship and workshop experiences.

## Fasting and Praying

The women were encouraged to practice the discipline of fasting and praying. Days were selected for the women to fast and pray collectively from 6:00 a.m., until 6:00 p.m., consuming eight glasses of water, herbal teas, and fruit juices. Most doctors recommend that everyone should drink at least eight glasses of water daily to help maintain healthy bodies.

## Foot Washing

The women, together with other female members of Mount Calvary who are not a part of "Sisters Sharing," gathered on a Friday evening for a special women's celebration worship service. After a "circle prayer" was completed, the women were instructed by the leader to take the hand of another woman in the circle, and move to a comfortable spot in the sanctuary, dining room, choir loft or choir room. Instructions were given to remove shoes (and stockings, if wanted) and to kneel at the woman's feet and anoint her feet with oil (distributed by the leader). Each woman ministered to her partner by praying a special prayer and anointing her feet. Herein we learned the importance of a servant's attitude, which in effect, was saying that no one is beneath us and there is no service I will not render for a sister (St. John 13:1-7).

## Prayer Partners

At this same Women's Celebration Worship Service, the women were asked to exchange telephone numbers with their partners and commit to pray together by telephone for the next seven days. The leader delivered a message entitled "Sisters of the Covenant." The theme of the message was the importance of bonding among women and making "covenants" or "commitments" to self, other women and God.

## Grooming The Feminine Temple

This workshop for women was held at Mount Calvary on a Saturday morning from 10 a.m. until 12 noon. A luncheon followed. This workshop was based on health awareness for the Christian woman. We engaged a female minister, The Reverend Wanda London of Campfield African Methodist Episcopal Church, Washington, D.C., to bring a message on "Inner and Outer Beauty."

Sisters Tracy Victor and Marie Jews, both registered nurses from the Mount Calvary Church family, distributed brochures on various health issues women face and gave lectures on the importance of regular pap smears, breast examinations and AIDS testing. Additional information was shared on diabetes, the hazards of smoking and other health issues relating to the Black woman. A question and answer period followed the lectures.

We invited women entrepreneurs to come display and sell their wares during the luncheon.

## Consultants

The United Theological Seminary also requires the candidate to select a group of consultants to assist in the development of the project. I chose the following persons:

**Dr. Peggy Wall** - an educator who presently serves as Administrator of the Bethel African Methodist Episcopal Church Christian School. Dr. Wall assists Mrs. Marlaa Hall Reid in teaching the women's Bible study group at Bethel. Dr. Wall conducts workshops and retreats for women; she is the founder of Inside Out Consultants.

**Dr. Eleanor Graham Bryant** - a prolific teacher of women's groups; she is founder and pastor of Agape Fellowship African Methodist Episcopal Church. Dr. Bryant has developed self-esteem programs for women through her doctoral studies.

**Mrs. Marlaa Hall Reid** - the coordinator and lead teacher of the women's Bible study group at Bethel African Methodist Episcopal Church. Mrs. Reid oversees the activities of over 500 women weekly. She also leads women's groups in workshops and seminars throughout the country.

**Dr. Renita Weems** - author of our main textbook, *"Just A Sister Away."* She lent her expertise in African-American women's studies to this project.

# A Look at the Model

The women of Towson and the Mount Calvary Church are a complex group. The church is over 100 years old, and many of the women have been a part of the church all of their lives. While there is a sizable number of senior women active in the church family, the majority of the women are between the ages of 21 and 60 years of age. The same statistics hold true for the men at Mount Calvary.

The difficulty I encountered with this project was that the women, mostly the Towson natives, have known each other all of their lives and most are related. I learned first hand at Mount Calvary that "familiarity breeds contempt." The women were "related," but as distant as the east is from the west as far as "relationships" were concerned. I discovered family feuds in process, feuds that had been passed down through generations. Class distinctions had been set up. Family and longevity in the church were steadfastly observed. I pastored a church that was classified as a "family church" but had little family spirit. The women, even relatives, were not very supportive of one another. This, of course, does not mean that none of the women supported other women, for I did observe that some of the younger women who had children without benefit of marriage were being supported by older women in their families. However, the support was so fragmented that it was difficult to determine who was really bonded with whom.

The majority of the households in the community are female headed households. Many of the children do not have the same father and many do not know their fathers. Some of the women have children by the same father who is married to neither woman. Some of the women have live-in boyfriends. Yet, many of these women depend on social services to support their households. Many of these women are not employed outside of the home. In the seven years I have served at Mount

Calvary, at least seven teenagers have had babies outside of wedlock. Some experienced multiple pregnancies; none appear to be in relationship with the fathers of their children. One can easily observe that in a church of this caliber it is sometimes difficult for a "sweet fellowship" to exist.

As the church has grown spiritually and numerically, the make-up of the women has changed dramatically. We now have more married couples in the church which means more male and female headed households and children with the benefit of both parents living in the home. Persons with different backgrounds, socially and educationally, are entering the Mount Calvary congregation. The church's composition and family make-up have changed as well. This influx of new members who have no previous history with the East Towson community has helped to dilute the traditional "family church" syndrome that shadowed the church for many years. The women who have come to Mount Calvary have helped demonstrate for the "old" members that women can work together inspite of existing barriers. I have observed that when a group expands, less attention is paid to individuals who formally may have been the main focus of the group. Adding new members who are not involved in the problem can help change the focus of former members. Love covers a multitude of sins. These new women have found a comfortable place among the original members and are working very effectively together on boards and organizations within the church.

Although the women would support other women or families in the church and community (through the Missionary Society) with traditional food baskets and occasional monetary assistance for rent, gas or electric, especially during Thanksgiving and Christmas, they had no habits of praying and fasting together or coming together to dialogue and share from the Word of God. In other words, there was very little "sisterhood" or "brotherhood" in the church community. After seven years as their pastor—teaching, preaching and modeling a different way of living out the reality of the beloved community, and the constant influx of new members—it is not uncommon now to see women and men off in a corner after service, holding hands, praying together or for women and men to bring another person to the altar for prayer. The people of Mount Calvary have been learning new ways of ministering to others through our worship services, Bible study sessions, prayer services and "Sisters Sharing" sessions. I take every opportunity possible to teach, by example, the necessity of ministering to one another. Many of Mount Calvary's men and women have regular prayer partners.

Over the past seven years, I have seen a new Mount Calvary evolve; and the people of God are learning to respect, love and support one another. Prayer has opened the door to fellowship and bonding at Mount Calvary. Beyond what the AME Discipline dictates, another wind is blowing that is not common in the African Methodist Episcopal Church.

Upon my arrival, I encountered a "traditional" African Methodist Episcopal Church. The people seemed to be more faithful to the denomination and it's traditions than they were to God. They followed the disciplinary procedures and worshipped like most "old-line" African Methodist Episcopal Churches – very quietly. Having served this congregation for seven years, I have sensed another wind blowing, another Spirit not found in the Discipline of the A.M.E. Church. The Mt. Calvary Church has become what traditionalists call "charismatic." That is, we do not adhere to the "AME Way." Rather, we *make a joyful noise unto the Lord.*" Old things are passing away; all things are becoming new!

The following pages consist of outlines of the sessions we shared over the twelve month period.

# The

# "Sisters Sharing"

# Sessions

## "Sisters Sharing"

## <u>Session One</u>

**Date:**         Saturday, November 6, 1992
**Time:**        8:00 a.m.
**Location:**   Reverend Lightner's home

**Teaching Aids:**  <u>The Holy Bible</u>

Dr. Renita Weems, <u>Just A Sister Away</u>
Chapter I, (Lura Media, San Diego,California, 1988)

T. D. Jakes, <u>Woman Thou Art Loosed</u>!
(Destiny Image Publishers, Shippensburg, PA., 1993)

Nell W. Mohney,
<u>Don't Put a Period Where God Put a Comma</u>,
(Dimensions for Living, South Nashville, TN., 1993)

**Method:**     Group Dialogue

**Subject:**    "A Mistress, A Maid, and No Mercy"
               (Sarah and Hagar)

**Scripture Lesson:**  Genesis 16:1-16; 21:1-21

**Lesson Aim:**   The purpose of this lesson was two-fold.

1. To demonstrate social rivalry between women of different social classes, races and ages in order to show how women exploit other women, especially where males are involved, while showing the human side of biblical women.

2. To share personally and to discuss in depth the the question the angel asks Hagar in Genesis 16:8, "Hagar, maid of Sarai, where have you come from and where are you going?"

# "Digging For The Gold"

I. Prayer Circle

II. Review of the Scripture Lesson

III. Exploring the Chapter

    1. Give a profile of the two women in this pericope of Scripture—Sarah and Hagar.
    2. What were the main issues raised in the Scripture?
    3. What were the main points raised by the author?
    4. What biblical truths did you personally learn from reading the Scripture and the textbook?
    5. How can these biblical truths be applied to your life?
    6. How might Sarah, Hagar and Abraham have handled this situation in a more positive manner?
    7. Who, if anyone, do you think was at fault?

IV. Review of Selected Questions From "Questions for Thought" from the text book

V. Personal Application

    1. Have you had conflict with another woman because of a love triangle? Discuss.
    2. How do you relate to women who are "beneath" you socially, economically, and educationally?
    3. How have you treated another woman's children (left in your care) as a result of your relationship with their father?
    4. What advice would you have given Sarah? Hagar?
    5. Were Sarah and Hagar enemies to each other?

**Note:** "Digging For The Gold" signified our purpose to go beneath the surface of the text and reveal the "hidden" meaning in the text in order to apply the lessons to our contemporary situations.

## Aunt Hagar's Children:

## "Where Are You Coming From, Where Are You Going?"

I. The Covenanting Process

    1. Can you be trusted with another woman's pain?
    2. The dangers of divulging information shared in confidence.
    3. Vow to keep one another's trust (talk only to that woman or to God about the other woman's pain).

II. Learning to Share Our Pain

    1. Voicing "undefined" pain.
    2. Voicing "unexpressed" pain.
    3. Releasing the pain.

III. Coming To Voice

Each woman has the opportunity to respond to the question, "Where Are You Coming From, Where Are You Going?" (See Appendix A)

**NOTE:** The "Sisters Sharing" group utilized two additional sessions with this lesson in order to allow each woman adequate time to share her past, which included the painful places in her life as well as the joyful places. It also gave each woman the opportunity to look at what she was trying to accomplish in her life.

I feel that the bonding process began at this point in the program.

## "Sisters Sharing"

### Session Two

**Date:**            Saturday, December 4, 1992

**Time:**            8:00 a.m.

**Location:**        Reverend Lightner's home

**Teaching Aids:**   The Holy Bible

Dr. Renita Weems, Just A Sister Away Chapter I,
(Lura Media, San Diego, California, 1988).

Robin Norwood, Women Who Love Too Much
(New York, New York, Pocket Books, 1985).

T. D. Jakes, Woman Thou Art Loosed!
(Destiny Image Publishers, Shippensburg, PA.,1993).

Evelyn Christenson, Lord, Change Me
(Wheaton, Illinois, Victor Books, 1987).

**Method:**          Group Dialogue and Individual Sharing

**Subject:**         Aunt Hagar's Children: "Where Are You Coming
From, Where Are You Going?"

**Scripture Lesson:** Genesis 16:1-16; 2:11-21

**Lesson Aim:** To encourage women to share personally and to discuss in depth the question the angel asks Hagar in Genesis 16:8, "Hagar, maid of Sarai, where have you come from, and where are you going?"

**Note:** This session was carried over to next month in order to allow each woman an opportunity to share her story.

# Aunt Hagar's Children:

## "Where Are You Coming From, Where Are You Going?"

I.  Circle Prayer

II.  Review of the Scripture Lesson

III.  The Covenanting Process Reviewed

1.  Can you be trusted with another woman's pain?
2.  The dangers of divulging information shared in confidence.
3.  Vow to keep one another's trust (talk only to that woman or to God about the other woman's pain).

IV.  Learning to Share Our Pain

1.  Voicing "undefined" pain.
2.  Voicing "unexpressed" pain.
3.  Releasing the pain.

V.  Coming To Voice

Each woman has the opportunity to respond to the question, "Where Are You Coming From, Where Are You Going?"

VI.  Instructions and Closing Prayer Circle

## "Sisters Sharing"

## <u>Session Three</u>

**Date:**            Saturday, January 8, 1993

**Time:**            8:00 a.m.

**Location:**        Sister Ursula Slade's home

**Teaching Aids:**   The Holy Bible

Dr. Renita Weems, Just A Sister Away
Chapter I, (Lura Media, San Diego, CA, 1988).

Robin Norwood, Women Who Love Too Much
(New York, New York, Pocket Books, 1985).

T. D. Jakes, Woman Thou Art Loosed!
(Destiny Image Publishers, Shippensburg, PA.,1993).

Evelyn Christenson, Lord, Change Me,
(Wheaton, Illinois, Victor Books, 1987).

**Method:**          Group Dialogue and Individual Sharing

**Subject:**         Aunt Hagar's Children: Where Are You Coming
From, Where Are You Going?"

**Scripture Lesson:**  Genesis 16:8; 2:11-21

**Lesson Aim:**  To encourage women to share personally and to discuss in depth the question the angel asks Hagar in Genesis 16:8, "Hagar, maid of Sarai, where have you come from, and where are you going?"

**Note:**  This lesson is continued from previous session in order to allow each woman time to share her story.

## Aunt Hagar's Children:

## "Where Are You Coming From, Where Are You Going?"

I. Circle Prayer

II. Review of the Scripture Lesson

III. The Covenanting Process Reviewed

    1. Can you be trusted with another woman's pain?
    2. The dangers of divulging information shared in confidence.
    3. Vow to keep one another's trust (talk only to that woman or to God about the other woman's pain).

IV. Learning to Share Our Pain

    1. Voicing "undefined" pain.
    2. Voicing "unexpressed" pain.
    3. Releasing the pain.

V. Coming To Voice

    Each woman has the opportunity to respond to the question, "Where Are You Coming From, Where Are You Going?"

VI. Instructions and Closing Prayer Circle

## "Sisters Sharing"

### Session Four

**Date:**            Saturday, February 6, 1993

**Time:**            8:00 a.m.

**Location:**        Reverend Lightner's home

**Teaching Aids:**   The Holy Bible

Dr. Renita Weems, Just A Sister Away
Chapter II, (Lura Media, San Diego, CA., 1988).

Robin Norwood, Women Who Love Too Much
(New York, New York, Pocket Books, 1985).

T. D. Jakes, Woman Thou Art Loosed!
(Destiny Image Publishers, Shippensburg, PA.,1993).

Evelyn Christenson, Lord, Change Me
(Wheaton, Illinois, Victor Books, 1987).

Jean Lush,
The Emotional Phases of A Woman's Life,
(Fleming H. Powell Co., Tarrytown, N.Y., 1987).

**Method:**          Group Discussion and Dialogue

**Subject:**         "Blessed Be The Tie That Binds" (Naomi and Ruth)

**Scripture Lesson:** The Book of Ruth

**Lesson Aim:** To help women understand the importance of woman to woman friendships without regard to age. To help women understand the importance of making covenants with other women to stick with each other through hard times. To view the danger of being forced to choose between male and female relationships.

76

# "Digging For The Gold"

I. Prayer Circle

II. Review of the Scripture Lesson

III. Exploring the Chapter

1. Give a profile of the three women in this pericope, Naomi, Ruth and Orpah.
2. What were the main issues raised in the pericope?
3. What were the main points raised by the author?
4. What biblical truths did you personally learn from reading the periscope and the textbooks?
5. Was Ruth imposing her friendship upon Naomi?
6. Why did Naomi reject Ruth and Orpah?
7. Describe an event that caused you to grieve. What blessings did you receive in the midst of your grief?

IV. Review of Selected Questions From "Questions For Thought" from the text book

V. Personal Application

1. What does true friendship mean to you? Describe your best friend.
2. What does the phrase, "My Sister's Keeper" mean to you personally?
3. What kind of friend do you feel you are to other women?
4. Are you more loyal to males than to females?
5. Do you relate well to women in other age groups?
6. Have you ever been rejected by a friend or relative?
7. What did Ruth's covenant with Naomi (1:16) mean to you personally?
8. Would you classify yourself as Ruth, Naomi or Orpah?
9. Have you ever been forced to choose between the friendship of a man and another woman?
10. What advice would you have given Ruth, Naomi and/or Orpah?

# "Sisters Sharing" Prayer Luncheon Participation

### March 6, 1993  -  11:00 a.m.
### Brown's Memorial Baptist Church, Baltimore, Maryland

Guest preacher was The Reverend Ann Farrar Lightner. "Sisters Sharing" group accompanied the leader in lieu of our regular session. The women met and fellowshipped with women of the Brown Memorial Baptist Church.

**Scripture Lesson:** II Kings 5:2-3  -  **Sermon Title:** "I've Got The Power."

**Text:** "And the Syrians had gone out by companies, and had brought away captive out of the land of Israel a little maid; and she waited on Naaman's wife. And she said unto her mistress, Would God my lord were with the prophet that is in Samaria! for he would recover him of his leprosy."

**Thesis:** Many women feel that because of their circumstances or who they are, that they are powerless to make a positive impact on the lives of other women and people in general.

**Proposition:** Women who may not have power or position in society or government have power to be a positive force in this world no matter what their particular circumstances. The "little maid" in this scripture lesson is proof of this. Women have power to impact the lives of others in at least three specific ways:

1. I've Got the Power to Love
   * Love my oppressor, my enemy
   * Love inspite of my personal circumstances
2. I've Got the Power to Liberate
   * My words or advice can lead another to freedom
   * Point people to Jesus, the healer and liberator
3. I've Got the Power to Lift
   * Encouragement lifts people (pouring courage into others)
   * Never look down on another woman; find ways to lift her up. Someone helped you when you needed a lift
   * Lift as you climb

**Conclusion:** This "little maid" had no name. All that we know of her is given in a mere twenty words in the Bible. But because she used what she had, her knowledge of the prophet in Israel, to help someone else, lives were changed and she no doubt reaped blessings in return. The Holy Spirit will enable you - to Love - to Liberate - to Lift.

**Note:** The women had opportunity to dialogue about this message in the April session which dealt with women's relationships as portrayed by Ruth and Naomi.

## "Sisters Sharing"

### Session Five

**Date:**              Saturday, April 6, 1993

**Time:**              8:00 a.m.

**Location:**          Reverend Lightner's home

**Teaching Aids:**     The Holy Bible

                       Dr. Renita Weems, Just A Sister Away
                       Chapter II, (Lura Media, San Diego, CA., 1988).

                       T. D. Jakes, Woman Thou Art Loosed!
                       (Destiny Image Publishers, Shippensburg, PA.,1993).

**Method:**            Group Discussion and Dialogue

**Subject:**           "Blessed Be The Tie That Binds" (Naomi and Ruth)

**Scripture Lesson:** Ruth 3-4

**Lesson Aim:** To help women understand the complex nature of women's friendship. To demonstrate balance - Naomi is now helping Ruth while in the beginning Ruth set out to be a support to the "mourning" Naomi.

# "Digging For The Gold"

I. Prayer Circle

II. Review of the Scripture Lesson

III. Exploring the Chapter

    1. What changes do you observe about Naomi's character?
    2. What part does "purpose" play in her transformation?
    3. What specifically did she teach Ruth about
        a. survival
        b. getting a husband?
    4. What customs do we learn about courtship and marriage during that time? How do they differ from our customs?
    5. What final joy did Ruth bring to Naomi's life?

IV. Review of Selected Questions from "Questions For Thought" from the textbook

V. Personal Application

    1. What, if anything, did you learn about commitment?
    2. Have you ever lost a woman friend because of a marriage or romantic relationship?
    3. How do you handle friends who always put men before your friendship?
    4. Have you ever had to be a "Ruth" and carry the load in a friendship? If yes, how did you handle the non-reciprocal friendship?
    5. What advice would you give a younger woman who is desirous of marriage?

# Mount Calvary African Methodist Episcopal Church
### 300 Eudowood Lane
### Towson, Maryland
### Reverend Ann Farrar Lightner, Pastor

### May 7, 1993
### 10:00 a.m. - 12:00 p.m.

### "Sisters Sharing" Workshop, Luncheon and Exhibition

### "Inner and Outer Beauty"

### **********

Moments of Praise and Worship . . . . . . . . . . . . . . Sister Patricia McCray

Opening Prayer . . . . . . . . . . . . . . . . . . . . . . . . Reverend Dorothy Gross

Scripture Reading . . . . . . . . . . . . . . . . . . . . . . . . . Sister April Burke
(I Corinthians 6:12-20)

Presentation of Speaker . . . . . . . . . . . . . Reverend Ann Farrar Lightner

Presentation "Inner and Outer Beauty" . . . . . . Reverend Wanda London
Associate Minister
Campbell African Methodist Episcopal Church
Washington, D.C.

Presentation of Speakers . . . . . . . . . . . . Reverend Ann Farrar Lightner

Presentation . . . . . . . . . . . . . . . . . . . . . . "Taking Care of the Temple"
Sister Tracy Victor, R.N.
Sister Marie Jews, R.N.

Question and Answer Period

Luncheon and Exhibits

Benediction . . . . . . . . . . . . . . . . . . . . . Reverend Ann Farrar Lightner

# "Sisters Sharing"

## Session Six

**Date:**           June 12, 1993

**Time:**           8:00 a.m.

**Location:**       Reverend Lightner's home

**Teaching Aids:**  The Holy Bible

Dr. Renita Weems, Just A Sister Away
Chapter II & III, (Lura Media, San Diego, CA 1988).

T. D. Jakes, Woman Thou Art Loosed!
(Destiny Image Publishers, Shippensburg, PA.,1993).

Evelyn Christenson, Lord, Change Me
(Wheaton, Illinois, Victor Books, 1987).

Alice Matthews, A Woman Jesus Can Teach
(Discovery House, Grand Rapids, MI, 1991).

**Method:**         Lecture by Reverend Lightner

**Subject:**        "Am I My Sister's Keeper?"

**Scripture Lesson:** Ruth 3-4

**Lesson Aim:** To share with the women the importance of women bonding with other women. To teach principals of friendship and "sisterhood" necessary to sustain relationships in difficult times. To teach certain methodology of mentoring as portrayed in the Book of Ruth and in I Timothy 1.

# AM I MY SISTER'S KEEPER?

### Reverend Ann Farrar Lightner, Leader

**Teaching Aids:**
                             The Book of Ruth
                             The First Letter to Timothy
                             Just A Sister Away, Dr. Renita Weems

A. Exploring the meaning of friendship; a friend comes around when the whole world has deserted you.

B. If you want to have a friend, learn how to first be a friend.

C. Object of friendship is to support, be supported and build one another up. Lift as you climb.

D. Friends make sacrifices one for the other. Friends do not always have strength to give.

E. Friends make covenants.

F. Friends do not betray other's confidence.

G. Friends do not bind friends and keep them from other friendships or relationships. Do not force people to choose.

H. True friendship must pass this test.

      1. love in action
      2. loyalty in trouble
      3. liberty to be what we are

# Mount Calvary African Methodist Episcopal Church
### 300 Eudowood Lane
### Towson, Maryland

### Reverend Ann Farrar Lightner, Pastor

### June 18, 1993
### 7:30 p.m.

### "Sisters Sharing"

### Women's Celebration Worship Service

### \*\*\*\*\*\*\*\*\*\*

Moments of Praise and Worship . . . . . . . . . . . . Sister Patricia McCray
and Sister Ursula Slade

Call to Worship . . . . . . . . . . . . . . . . . . . . . . . . . Sister Doris Jackson

Opening Hymn . . . . . . . . . . . . . . . . . . . . . . . . . "What A Fellowship"

Scripture Reading . . . . . . . . . . . . . . . . . . . . . . . Sister Yolanda Carroll
St. John 13:1-17

Prayer Circle . . . . . . . . . . . . . . . . . . All Women Form Circle for Prayer

Women Ministering to Women . . . . . . . . . . . . . Footwashing and Prayer

Women's Celebration Message . . . . . . . Rev. Ann Farrar Lightner, Pastor

### "Sisters of The Covenant"

Altar Prayer . . . . . . . . . . . . . . . . . . . . . . . . . . . Rev. Ann Farrar Lightner

Benediction . . . . . . . . . . . . . . . . . . . . . . . . . . . Rev. Ann Farrar Lightner

# "Sisters Sharing"

## Session Seven

**Date:**        Saturday, September 25, 1993

**Time:**        8:00 a.m.

**Place:**      Reverend Lightner's home

**Teaching Aids:** The Holy Bible

Dr. Renita Weems, Just A Sister Away
Chapter III, (Lura Media, San Diego, California,
1988).

Evelyn Christenson, Lord, Change Me
(Wheaton, Illinois, Victor Books, 1987).

Alice Matthews, A Woman Jesus Can Teach
(Discovery House, Grand Rapids, Michigan., 1991).

**Method:**    Group Discussion and Dialogue

**Subject:**    "My Sister's Keeper" (Martha and Mary)

**Scripture Lesson:** St. Luke 10:38-42; St. John 11:1-44 & 12:1-8

**Lesson Aim:** To demonstrate the similarities as well as differences in women's personalities, abilities and ambitions. To help women learn to respect one another's differences and chosen vocations and lifestyles.

# "Digging For The Gold"

I. Prayer Circle

II. Review of the Scripture Lesson

III. Exploring the Chapter

1. Give a profile of the two women in this pericope, Martha and Mary.
2. What were the main issues raised in the pericope?
3. What were the main points raised by the author?
4. What biblical truths did you personally learn from reading the Scripture and the chapter?

IV. Review of Selected Questions from "Questions For Thought" from the textbook

V. Personal Application

1. Have you had conflict with other women because of differences in priorities or work habits?
2. Do you and other women in your home or on your job find it difficult to work together?
3. What part does respect play in this story?
4. How do you think you would have reacted if you were in Martha's and/or Mary's place?
5. Can you remember a time you disrespected another women publicly?
6. Do you feel that Jesus appreciated Martha's gifts more than Mary's?
7. How do you differ from the women closest to you (mother, sister, friend, etc.)?

# "Sisters Sharing"

## Lesson Eight

**Date:**  October 2, 1993

**Time:**  8:00 a.m.

**Place:**  Reverend Lightner's home

**Teaching Aids:**  The Holy Bible

Dr. Renita Weems, Just A Sister Away
Chapter IV, (Lura Media, San Diego, CA., 1988).

T. D. Jakes, Woman Thou Art Loosed!
(Destiny Image, Shippensburg, PA., 1993).

Linda J. Hollis, Womanistcare Volume I
(WIWMI Publications, Evanston, Illinois, 1992).

**Method:**  Group Discussion and Dialogue

**Subject:**  "A Crying Shame"
(Jephthah's Daughter and the Mourning Women)

**Scripture Lesson:**  Judges 11:1-40

**Lesson Aim:**  To demonstrate the need for "sisters sharing," "mentoring," and "bonding" between women. This lesson will actually show women bearing one another's burdens. To emphasize the healing that can come from "mourning" or "crying." Also points out abuses afflicted upon women.

## "Digging For The Gold"

I. Prayer Circle

II. Review of the Scripture Lesson

III. Exploring the Chapter

    1. Give a profile of the main characters in this pericope. (Jephthah, Jephthah's daughter and the wailing woman).

    2. What were the main issues raised in this pericope?

    3. What were the main points raised by the author?

    4. What biblical truths did you personally learn from reading this pericope and the textbook? How can these be applied to your life?

    5. How was Jephthah's daughter abused in this story?

    6. Do you know any modern day Jephthah's? Explain.

    7. Have you had to come to the rescue of a woman who was being physically abused?

    8. What advice would you give a friend who was being

        a. verbally abused?

        b. physically abused?

    9. Have you ever been involved in an abusive relationship?

    10. What part does self esteem play in the part of a woman living in an abusive situation?

IV. Review of Selected Questions from "Questions For Thought" from the textbook

V. Personal Application

    1. How do you feel about Jephthah's daughter and the other "certain women" in the Bible being left in history without benefit of a name?

    2. How important are names for women in our society? Do you know the meaning of any African and African-American women's names?

    3. What cultural norms may have guided the decision of Jephthah's daughter to submit to her father's will?

    4. Is this story about abuse or is it about insensitivity? Is there a difference? Explain.

    5. How do you think you would have reacted if you were the woman in this story? How is today's woman different from biblical women in this instance?

    6. What women would you ask to go away with you in a mournful situation? What characteristics would you want these women to have?

# "Sisters Sharing"

## Lesson Nine

**Date:**              November 13, 1993

**Time:**              8:00 a.m.

**Location:**        Reverend Lightner's home

**Teaching Aids:**   The Holy Bible

Thomas N. Hart, The Art of Christian Listening (Paulist Press, New York, Ramsey 1980).

Muriel Solomon, What Do I Say When (Prentice Hall, New Jersey, 1988).

Ken Sande, Blessed Are The Peace Makers (Baker Book House, Grand Rapid, Michigan, 1992).

**Method:**          Lecture By Dr. Peggy Wall

**Subject:**         "Be Quick To Listen"

**Scripture Lesson:** James 1:19; Proverbs 18:13; 15:28; 2:1-2; 15:23; Psalms 141:15

**Lesson Aim:** To teach women the importance of developing good listening skills as a tool for effective mentoring. Focus was on the elements of effective listening and the importance of love in listening.

# "Be Quick To Listen ..!"

I. Listening defined (What is it?) (James 1:19)
    A. a communication skill that requires practice
    B. a communication skill that requires understanding
    C. a communication skill that requires compassion

II. Elements of Effective Listening
    A. Waiting before answering (Proverbs 18:13)
        1. prevents listener from jumping to premature conclusions
        2. disciplines listener not to interrupt while others speak
        3. helps listeners to be comfortable with silence
    B. Attending and concentrating on what is being said (Pr.15:28)
        1. keeps listener focused on speaker
        2. strengthens eye contact
        3. forces listener to eliminate distractions (t.v., music, radio)
        4. encourages positive body language (i.e., leaning forward to show interest, unfolding arms, nodding)
    C. Clarifying and understanding what has been communicated (Proverbs 2:1-2)
        1. strengthens questioning techniques (i.e., Are you saying...? I'm confused about... Can you give me an example?)
        2. strengthens hearing and thinking skills
    D. Reflecting, paraphrasing and/or summarizing in your own words (Proverbs 15:23)
        1. opens the door for further dialogue even in the midst of disagreement
        2. ensures speaker that the listener is listening
        3. diminishes the need for repetition
        4. slows down the pace of emotionally high conversations
    E. Agreeing - especially in pointing out personal errors (Ps14:13)
        1. encourages one to listen for truth
        2. minimizes the desire to blame others or focus on points of disagreement
        3. controls emotions and fosters genuine humility
        4. moves conversations in a more constructive direction

III. To Listen is to Love
    A. listening is time consuming
    B. listening can be painful
    C. listening may be spiritually hazardous
    D. listening is an act of love

## Other Models

Since her beginning, the African Methodist Episcopal Church, along with other denominations has placed strict gender role expectations on her members. These biblical patterns of male domination, sexism and patriarchal leadership still prevail in many churches. It seems most ironic that a denomination birthed as a result of opposition to racism and discrimination would in turn discriminate against her own - in this case, the female. Molefi Asante, a leading authority on Afrocentricity, believes that one cannot be both sexist and Afrocentric.

In spite of the proverbial "glass ceiling" that is yet the unspoken rule in the average Black church, women are steadily progressing in areas of church leadership. In the African Methodist Episcopal Church, for example, ministers' wives have demonstrated that women can be a tremendous asset to the life and ministries of the church when allowed to move beyond the "traditional" role of pastor's wife.

More often than not, I have observed that the pastor's wife does not take an active part in the overall planning and implementing of church programs. This varies of course, but usually the pastor does not include his wife in these important matters of the church. There are however, exceptions, as seen by the example of the following women:

> **Cecelia Williams Bryant** - serving with her husband, Reverend John R. Bryant, at Saint Paul and Bethel African Methodist Episcopal Churches.
> **Elaine McCollum Flake** - serving at Allen African Methodist Episcopal Church, Jamaica, New York, Reverend Floyd Flake, Pastor.
> **Barbara Austin Lucas** - serving at Bridge Street African Methodist Episcopal Church, Reverend Fred Lucas, Pastor.

**JoAnn Skaggs Browning** - serving at Ebenezer African Methodist Episcopal Church, Fort Washington, Maryland, Reverend Grainger Browning, Pastor.

**Jessica Kendall Ingram** - serving at Oak Grove African Methodist Episcopal Church, Detroit, Michigan, Reverend Gregory Ingram, Pastor.

**Marlaa Hall Reid** - serving at Bethel African Methodist Episcopal Church, Baltimore, Maryland, Reverend Frank Madison Reid, III, Pastor.

These women, and many others, have brought new life and exciting ministries to their pastor/husband's churches by developing vibrant women's ministries, most of which started with a simple weekly women's Bible study group and have grown to annual women's retreats, prayer breakfasts, women's national and international conferences and a host of weekly ministries designed to meet the needs of the majority of their congregations—women—at these local churches.

It is fascinating to watch God grow women leaders in organized churches. These women were not ordained ministers when they married their pastor/husbands. Most of them had not even heard a call from God. However, while mentoring God's women in the church, God called some of them to preach the word, and these women are being used on an even higher level. They preach, teach, and assist with the overall planning of the church.

With the exception of Marlaa Hall Reid, all have accepted the call to preach, completed seminary and have been ordained. This is not to infer that all women who work in the church will necessarily be called of God to preach. Marlaa Hall Reid speaks and teaches at churches around the country and is an excellent example of the fact that a woman does not have to be ordained in order to be an effective Christian leader.

The fruit of these ministries speaks for itself. Two of these women, Jessica Kendall Ingram and Elaine McCollum Flake, are scholars at United Theological Seminary in the Doctorate of Ministry program. Reverends Lucas and Browning have both completed Doctorate of Ministry programs at other seminaries. Reverend Bryant is now serving as Missionary Supervisor of the Tenth Episcopal District of the African Methodist Episcopal Church, (the state of Texas) with her husband, Bishop John R. Bryant. Marlaa Hall Reid ministers to approximately 500 women weekly at Bethel African Methodist Episcopal Church. Marlaa does not feel called to the ordained ministry although she acknowledges that God has called her to ministry, to preach and to teach God's word. Marlaa also organizes the Annual Women's Day choir consisting of some 300 voices.

The fruit of the ministries of these women, serving with their husbands, proves that women can be a tremendous asset to their husbands/pastors. There is no valid need to fear that women are going to "take over" their husband's churches. Pastors' wives generally respect and support the role of their husbands as "pastor of the church." Both pastor and wife should be directed by God in order for the ministry to prosper. There is no room for competition. It is all to be done to the glory of God for kingdom building.

Yet there are some gifted and talented women who happen to be pastor's wives, who are sitting on the second row looking like "queens," who need to be taken off their pedestals and let loose in the congregation to become mentors to the women God has placed in their midst. I write this in detail for two specific reasons:

1. In hopes that some pastor will be led to allow his wife to use her gifts and talents in the church without fear that she will become "rebellious" (like Queen Vashti in Esther 1:1-12).

2. In hopes that some preacher's wife, daughter, sister or mother will be directed by God to break free from the "traditional" role of sitting on the second row looking like a "queen" or "first lady" or simply directing the choir or playing for the choir (which are worthwhile ministries) to be used of God "for such a time as this."

Women are hungry for ministry; and, I might insert a word of caution. If women's ministries are not developed in local churches, women will search out a church that offers what they need.

# CHAPTER FIVE

## SUMMARY AND CONCLUSIONS

### PERSONAL OBSERVATIONS

The "Sisters Sharing" group has had several opportunities to mentor other women both from our group and outside the group. Their willingness to go to other women (without my intervention) and support these women demonstrates their growth and confidence in both themselves and God. They are no longer afraid to reach out and risk being a "sister" to someone who is in pain and in need of a "sister."

Several women from within our "Sisters Sharing" group have experienced trials and tribulations during this journey and found love and support from "sisters" within the group:

* a mother's son was shot and killed one year after she buried another son;
* two women's marriages broke up; they have both reconciled with their husbands;
* one woman suffered a miscarriage;
* one woman's husband is a drug abuser.

Through all of these situations, the women in the group have supported the woman in pain and helped her through the dark night of the soul. I witnessed bonding taking place among the women. They began to care sincerely about what was happening in the lives of other women in the group. This was exhibited in our prayer circle when prayers were lifted. The women earnestly prayed one for the other.

Trust was built. During the sessions where we shared our personal experiences, "Where Are you Coming From, Where Are you Going?" the women took a vow to keep one another's confidence and not share another's story outside of the group except with God in prayer. To date, I have had no reports of broken trust. No woman has left the group because of another woman's insensitivity.

Several members of the group were new members at Mount Calvary when we started the sessions. Their participation in the "Sisters Sharing" sessions accelerated their acceptance by other women in the church. They were benefited by having the opportunity to get to know several members of the congregation on a personal level during the early stages of their involvement with the church. I have seen members join who, for years, have not had any personal interaction with other members of the congregation.

However, the members of "Sisters Sharing" have become a part of the full life of the church and are serving in other capacities such as the usher board, choirs and Sunday School. Most attend our weekly Bible study. I might add that these women are also tithers.

## LEADERSHIP SKILLS DEMONSTRATED

In the beginning of the "Sisters Sharing" sessions, the women were not willing to meet and work through the lessons without the leader's presence. However, toward the end of our sessions, the women had divided themselves into teams and were meeting at their own homes preparing for the upcoming lessons. This, for me, is an indication of the growth of the women, and that they have successfully bonded in love and fellowship and feel comfortable exploring the Word of God without an "expert" present. Note that the leader did not mandate these private group sessions.

The women are planning a worship celebration for the participants of "Sisters Sharing," their families and friends for February 1994. Each woman will receive a certificate from the leader in commemoration of this year long journey. The women will plan and carry out every aspect of the service without the leader directing them. This would not have happened one year ago!

I stated earlier in the "Why The Model Was Developed" section that during my early "Sisters Sharing" session with the young females of the church, the adult females participated in order that they might be a part of the sessions; they did not demonstrate very much leadership ability in terms of "program development" or "mentoring" the younger women. Based on the women's performance in these "Sisters Sharing" sessions and watching them in other roles in the church, I feel that many of them are now ready to take on the responsibility of designing and implementing a program for our younger sisters. Of course, I would supervise the effort, but I feel confident that the group is now ready for the task.

## WALK A MILE IN MY SHOES

The women have, by their own testimonies, gained a new level of respect for other women as a result of our journey together. The women have learned to listen and hear beyond what another woman is able to articulate. Compassion is demonstrated in the group. The women have become more accepting of other women's faults and differences. The Bible study lessons helped them to see the value of putting ourselves in another woman's place before judging or condemning her.

## GREATER SELF-CONFIDENCE

Women in the "Sisters Sharing" group are beginning to realize the gifts and talents they hold in their bosom; they are anxious to develop and use them for God's glory. Tracy is a registered nurse and is preparing to enroll in medical school; Yolonda, Karen and Ornita have enrolled in local colleges and are working toward undergraduate degrees. Rosemary is anticipating enrollment at a local university to pursue a Doctorate Degree.

## OBSTACLES

Space was a slight problem. The group met at my home primarily for purposes of intimacy and comfort, but also because there was no available space at the church.

Because of our time constraints, we were often not able to complete much of the material on our outlines. It would be advantageous to have longer sessions in order for more of the material to be covered.

Child care was also a concern. Many of the women had to bring young children with them to the sessions. This meant that often they could not give their undivided attention to the lessons and dialogue.

We will need to secure a sitter to relieve the mothers during the sessions. However, the fact that the women pressed their way, even in the dead of winter, to these early morning sessions demonstrated their need for "Sisters Sharing."

## WHERE DO WE GO FROM HERE?

Word of this project has spread throughout Baltimore and vicinity. One of the reasons for the news spreading is that wherever I have been called upon to deliver messages, I lift up the results of this ministry. Another reason is that the women themselves are excited and are talking about it in their circles.

As a result of the positive impact it has had on Mount Calvary's women and other women involved in the project, both pastors and lay persons have requested that I share the findings of this project. I have also had several requests to serve as a consultant and develop similar programs for other pastors. One such request came from a female minister from a Baptist church in New Jersey. She came to observe one of our sessions and following her visit, requested that I come to New Jersey and train leaders to start a similar program for the women. Beyond the effect that this project has had on women, the men of Mount Calvary have requested that I assist in setting up a "Brothers Sharing" program. The planning is already underway.

This first segment of "Sisters Sharing" is near completion. The group decided that it would be detrimental for this initial group to try to integrate with a new group of women since they have already bonded. I have a list of new women who want to become a part of "Sisters Sharing." (After a six month period of time had gone by, we stopped enrollment in the first session). This new group will, no doubt, be larger and will meet on a bi-monthly basis rather than monthly. The difference will be that this leader will not assume the sole responsibility of leading and hosting the group sessions. The women from the initial "Sisters Sharing" group will assist; women who have been mentored and taught to mentor will now be available to mentor others.

The answers to the questions derived from the lessons demonstrated the women's growth and development as Christians and women willing and better prepared to be mentors to others.

Their answers and observations bespoke of change and growth. They demonstrated their ability to "dig for the gold"— diligently search the Scriptures and apply them to their lives as African-American women—outside the presence of the leader. The responses also demonstrate these womens' desire and ability to become mentors. Further, the members of "Sisters Sharing" have agreed to reorganize younger females at Mount Calvary (ages 12-18) and design a more effective program to mentor younger sisters.

In order to both summarize our discussions and access the women's level of understanding of the materials covered, the leader designed review questions for the women to answer. Following is a sample of the summary questions from the "EXIT INTERVIEW." The women divided themselves into teams and answered the questions collectively.

A <u>verbatim</u> summary of these discussions follows the sample questions.

## Women's Group Summary

## of

## "Just A Sister Away"

## Chapters 1, 2, 3 and 4

A. Review of the Chapter

> ★ What were the main issues raised in the group's discussion?
> ★ What main points were the author trying to get across?
> ★ What were the pertinent points of the group discussion?
> ★ What did you personally learn from the lesson?
> ★ Will these lessons change or shape your relationships with other women? If yes, can you describe and give examples?

B. What conclusions were drawn by:

> 1. Dr. Renita Weems?
> 2. The "Sisters Sharing" group?
> 3. You?

# "Just A Sister Away"

## Summary of Chapter One

## "A Mistress, A Maid, and No Mercy"

### (Hagar and Sarah)

### <u>Team One</u>

A.  Main Issues Raised In Group Discussion:

> ★ Jealousy, ethnic prejudice and not submitting to God's will. A woman's personal worth and value must be considered.

Main points raised by the author:

> ★ Showing how women hurt each other
> ★ Sisterhood often goes out of the window when involving a man
> ★ Self-esteem should not be determined by class or by another person's perception of a woman

Pertinent points of group discussion:

> ★ Pain and our reaction to pain
> ★ Determining our focus
> ★ Co-dependency

What we personally learned from the lesson:

| | |
|---|---|
| **Nancy** | It caused me to reflect on how much Sarah and Hagar I have in me, and to question if Abraham lives at my house. |
| **Nancy** | I focused on myself, and am attempting to redirect my life. I would like to follow a path that is socially and spiritually positive. |
| **Yolonda** | I learned I had not grown so much as I thought. It was time to redirect my life. I could not stay complacent. I can't continue to accept complacency as a way of life. |

Will these lessons change or shape your relationships with other women?

|  |  |
|---|---|
| **Norma:** | Yes it will. I have become a better witness and mentor. |
| **Nancy:** | Yes it did. It has given me the strength to help women without regard to their reactions. |
| **Yolonda:** | The lessons have changed my life. I have become softer and more compassionate in my dealings with other women. |

B. Conclusions:

1.  Given the opportunity we don't always help each other. As women, we should have more compassion for each other. We need to move beyond jealousy and reach out to one another.

2.  The group was in agreement with Dr. Weems. We also decided to become more supportive of other women.

3.  **Nancy:** I love my sisters. I can identify with my sisters. I want to put that love and identity into action.
    **Yolonda:** It is a joy to be a woman. Together, we can make each other stronger.
    **Norma:** It is wonderful to have a support group of other women. Also, to be a support to other women.

# "Just A Sister Away"

## Summary of Chapter Two

### "Blessed Be The Tie That Binds"
### Ruth and Naomi

### Team Two

A. Main Issues Raised in Group Discussion:

- ★ Naomi's bitterness
- ★ Ruth's commitment to Naomi
- ★ Ruth's love for Naomi
- ★ Death of Naomi's family
- ★ Friendship between Ruth and Naomi
- ★ Naomi is destitute

B. Main points raised by the author:

- ★ The true meaning of family; not just husband and children; includes all who live together and love and take care of each other.
- ★ The true meaning of commitment; which means to have an emotional obligation to someone.
- ★ The true meaning of friendship; which is to be loyal, under-standing, and be nonjudgmental
- ★ The true meaning of love; which is the unselfish, loyal and benevolent concern for the good of another.

C. Pertinent points of group discussion:

- ★ Ruth's commitment to Naomi; her desire to take care of Naomi.
- ★ Women being friends, opening up to one another, showing pain, and being a mentor to one another.

D. What we personally learned from the lesson
   (Group did not submit answers)

Will these lessons change or shape your relationships with other women? If yes, can you describe and give examples?

**Shawnise:** Yes, I will be more cautious about who claims to be my friend. I will not be a friend to someone who really doesn't care about me, just so I will have a friend. I will be open enough to let a new friend in.

**Sharon:** No, because I have always empathized with other women.

**Pat:** Yes, it has given me a new definition of friendship. Before I would look for friends just to be in the "in crowd." I know the true meaning of friendship is to be myself.

E. Conclusions

1. Conclusions drawn by Dr. Weems:

The good fortune of one woman is not the misfortune of another. Naomi showed Ruth what to do to get a husband, and Ruth's good fortune to remarry did not cause her to be selfish and forget about Naomi's needs. Naomi needed love, family and friendship in her life.

Ruth was intentional to preserve her friendship with Naomi. Ruth did not want their friendship to die just because their husbands were dead.

2. Conclusions drawn by the "Sisters Sharing" group:

Women need to learn how to be friends, how to open up to one another, how to listen and not judge one another, how to show pain, and how to mentor one another.

3. Conclusions drawn by me:

**Sharon:** Women should be more understanding and willing to come to the aid of other women.

**Shawnise:** To look deep inside myself and realize who my true friends are.

**Pat:** To be unselfish enough to sacrifice what I think would be the good life in order to get someone else started. Ruth was sympathetic enough to help Naomi find a reason for living instead of deserting her.

## "Just A Sister Away"

### Summary of Chapter Three

### "My Sister's Keeper"
### (Martha and Mary)

### <u>Team Three</u>

A. Main Issues Raised In Group Discussion:

★ All women are different, however, women must still respect other women when their ways may not be the same as ours.

★ Some women take other women for granted, especially when women have different talents—women assume the other person will always perform their special "talent."

★ Women must accept other women for what they are and accept their positions in life. For example, their beliefs and habits and remember no one is perfect; everyone makes mistakes.

★ Women are more critical of a sister, more so than a man. A woman will quickly judge another sister; however, a man will be excused for one reason or another.

★ You must be there for a woman even when her problems are continuous. For example, when a woman continues to remain in an unhappy and abusive relationship, knowing there is a better way for her, you must let her know you are there for her. That doesn't mean you have to be totally involved in the problem; just be a good listener.

★ Women are more tolerant of other women who are close to them (mothers, daughters, sisters and nieces), and they must learn to do the same for others.

★ Every job is important - especially when it's for the Lord.

★ Women make too many assumptions before they actually talk to people. Some women appear to be different from the way they really are—you have to talk to them to find out.

★ Young women need strong role models to help them in this world.

B. Conclusions:

**April:** Accepting women for who they are is very important. Women sometimes put too many demands and expectations on other women. Also our values and morals are completely out of place. Women are now too concerned with their hair, nails, clothes and being sexually active more than their health, education, and just being themselves. Women need to be reminded that no matter what their situation may be they are special, and that they can make a difference in the world.

Will these lessons change or shape your relationship with other women? If yes, can you describe or give one or two examples.

**Ursula:** Yes, the lesson of Martha and Mary will change my relationship with other women. I have a habit of expecting a lot out of my women friends. I get upset easily when they do not live up to my expectations. I must learn to accept and not try to change them.

Example: When I try to encourage a friend of mine that she could make it without being in a dead-end relationship, she continues to complain to me but won't do anything to try to change. I must continue to be there for her and not avoid her. Each of us is blessed with certain gifts. These gifts must be used and nourished. We must love each sister even when they're not at our level of growth.

**Keionna:** Yes. I will no longer take other women or their positions for granted. Each job is important, but I would rather sit and learn. I am not the type to be in a leadership position. I like for things to be in place, but I have grown accustomed to having others take care of the details, i.e., my mother.

# "Just A Sister Away"

## Summary of Chapter Four

### "A Crying Shame"
### Jephthah's Daughter

### <u>Team Four</u>

A. Main Issues Raised By The Group:

   ★ How men use and abuse women for their own purposes, glory, power. Women end up suffering for men.
   ★ How low self-esteem affects men;
   ★ Women sympathized with other women (weeping);
   ★ Different responses today's women might have;

B. Main points of the author:

   ★ Women need to stick together and support one another during their valley periods.
   ★ We need to weep for one another.
   ★ Women should know available resources for women in crises.

C. Pertinent points of group discussion:

   ★ Women need to weep more for other women and support them.
   ★ We need to teach women that they are "too good" to be mistreated and abused by men.
   ★ Also, women should give loving advice to other women
   ★ Teach women the value of self-worth

D. What was personally learned from the lesson?

   We all agreed that we need to be more responsive to other women and take time to listen to them, as well as weep more for them and in some cases, begin to weep for them.

# SISTERS SHARING

## Mount Calvary African Methodist Episcopal Church

### EXIT INTERVIEW - QUESTIONS

1. Will these sessions change or shape your relationships with other women? Explain.

2. Do you feel better equipped to counsel/mentor another woman? Explain.

3. Have you begun putting your mentoring skills into practice? Explain.

4. Do you feel any differently about yourself as a "sister" having participated in "Sisters Sharing?" Explain.

5. Do you think every local church should have a group similar to "Sisters Sharing?" Explain.

6. If another "Sisters Sharing" group was formed, would you feel comfortable being a leader of the group? Explain.

Note:    The women's <u>verbatim</u> responses to the above questions follow.

# SISTERS SHARING

# EXIT INTERVIEWS

## ★ ANSWERS ★

## Patricia

1. A change in my attitude towards the pain of other women will surely be made. I believe I will be better able to show more compassion than before, and to listen to their concerns without giving my opinion. I'll be more encouraging, where before I was a bit sanctimonious in my actions.

2. Yes, I feel better equipped; my listening skills have become attuned to what is being said by actions instead of words. I am not saying I will become a professional counselor, but I will strive to be a professional confidante.

3. Not yet, but I am open for the opportunity.

4. Anytime I am involved in a Bible study/fellowship/retreat scenario geared toward the spiritual maturing of women, I always come away not only feeling differently, but looking differently at what I consider tragic or no way out situations. I then consider myself blessed to be granted the opportunity to share with other women, which gives way to healing. When we share the valley experiences that we have had in our lives, and then experience deliverance, I then am reassured that God is able.

5. Yes. There can never be enough fellowships specifically concentrated on self-esteem building, active Bible study groups, and the opportunity to interact with other women. We as women know that we all are pressing through trial and tribulation. We often times feel as though we are the only ones going through the valley, but when we fellowship with other women and learn that they too have suffered and are going through a healing process, we then learn to appreciate our valley experience, and allow God to heal us.

6. Yes. With the training that has occurred in this group and the opportunity to learn what areas need addressing, being comfortable is not a commodity but a necessity. So when do we begin?

## Shawnise

1. Yes, these sessions will and have helped to shape my relationships with other women. I have learned that I do not have to beg any woman to be my friend. I learned that if a woman does not want to be my friend, it doesn't mean something is wrong with me. I have friends in the Sisters Sharing group

that I can count on for support. I feel good about being involved in the group.

2. Yes. I feel better equipped to council/mentor other women. I do feel that I need more training.

3. Yes. There are two women in particular that I listen to and try to recommend solutions regarding their personal and job related problems.

4. Yes. I feel more willing to share my pains, and to thank God for everything He has done for me.

5. Yes. Women need other women. Women need to know that other women share their pain and that they are not alone.

6. Yes. I would feel comfortable being a leader of the group.

## Ursula

1. These sessions have changed my relationships with other women because I am better able to sympathize with women going through crises. These sessions have shaped my relationships with other women because I can accept them as they are and not expect more than they are willing to give.

2. I feel better equipped to mentor other women because I have grown spiritually. Before I give any advice, I always pray and seek God's direction. This was not true of me before "Sisters Sharing."

3. I have begun to put my mentoring skills into practice on my job. I supervise 13 women from different walks of life. I use what I have learned in "Sisters Sharing" to give direction to these women.

4. Because of my participation in "Sisters Sharing," I am able to "give more of myself" when another sister is in need. In this "Sisters Sharing" group I am able to show my weaker side and not be criticized.

5. Every church should have a group like "Sisters Sharing." There is a need for women to get together, share and not feel as though they have to be alone.

6. I do not feel comfortable being sole leader of a "Sisters Sharing" group at this time. When my listening skills improve, I will feel more equipped.

## Tracy

1. Yes. Sisters Sharing has made me realize what the word sister really stands for - trust, understanding, love, listening and being real with one another. These sessions have enabled me to go into female relationships with the above qualities, and be a true sister.

2. Yes. I feel I have better listening skills. I know who I am and am not ashamed of where I came from; it allows me to be a more effective mentor.

3. Yes. I deal with women on a daily basis at work. I have the opportunity to share with sisters, listen to sisters, and at times pray with them. I encourage

the young ladies to find a positive insight about their lives and look up.

4. Being an only daughter, I find myself with the best sisters God could give anyone. I feel comfortable saying what's on my mind, not having to worry about what others think or how it will sound. I feel secure in my sisters.

5. Yes. If God's women would learn to be "real sisters" to one another, the body of Christ will grow stronger in numbers and faith.

6. Not at this time. I am being taught and do not feel completely comfortable leading, but I do feel I have leadership skills and one day I do plan on leading a "Sisters Sharing" group if it be the will of God.

## Rosemary

1. The sessions have enabled me to become more sensitive to another woman's stories. We can sometimes overlook the needs of our sisters due to our being focused on our own needs. As a result of "Sisters Sharing," I have grown as a woman and would like to challenge other women to grow.

2. I feel better equipped to counsel women of the faith because "Sisters Sharing" was comprised of Christian women. As Christians, we share a bond and a commonality unlike groups comprised of non-Christian women. As a Christian, I feel it was easier to share with my sisters some of the struggles that are unique to Christian women. Through the scriptural references and experiences shared, I am equipped to counsel and/or mentor other women.

3. I have begun to discuss issues that I once felt uncomfortable discussing with another woman. Through mentoring we must be able to disclose our experiences and share of ourselves.

4. After participating in "Sisters Sharing," I feel that I am unique and special as a woman. I feel that my story is important. This group has reinforced and validated my exquisiteness as a woman.

5. Yes. I think every local church should have a group similar to "Sisters Sharing." There are things that women need to share with other women. Through these groups we can express these issues in a "safe" environment.

6. If another "Sisters Sharing" group was formed, I would feel comfortable being a leader because we have built a foundation of trust and openness.

## Keionna

1. Yes. It taught me to be a better listener and friend.

2. Yes. I am in the process of developing my listening skills. This will enable me to mentor other women.

3. I'm trying. When someone calls to tell me about their problem or to ask advice, I try not to interrupt and share my problems. I am more sensitive now.

4. Yes. I have learned the real definition of what a sister is. I have women whom I thought were my true friends, but found out that they were not. But I have some true friends that I took for granted.

5. Yes. Women need to be closer in order to help one another.

6. Not right now, I am still in the process of developing my listening skills which I feel are important to be a good leader.

## Myrtice

1. Yes. It allows me to be able to express myself with other women, and it allows me to be able to understand how they feel.

2. Yes. To mentor ... because I can do that with the parents on my job. I can share with them things I have experienced and how my experiences can help them. Most of my parents are younger.

3. Yes. On my job with parent conferences and younger family members.

4. Yes. Before, I wouldn't talk to people; now can I talk about my problems with women I trust.

5. Yes. I think every local church should encourage the young and older women to participate in things together.

6. It would depend on the group. If the group was made up of women I know, I would feel more comfortable. Otherwise, I wouldn't feel comfortable.

## Norma

1. Yes. It gives me an opportunity to appreciate and understand where other women are coming from.

2. The few sessions I attended were very helpful. Because I missed some, I don't feel equipped to counsel other women.

3. Kind of. I always try to help others.

4. No.

5. Yes. Everybody needs someone else. It's nice to have a support group.

6. Yes. I have a lot to offer.

## IS THE BLACK CHURCH READY FOR
## A FEMALE MENTORING PROGRAM?

In the case of the African Methodist Episcopal Church, over 200 years have passed, and the church has not yet fully recognized the particular needs of its majority population - women. In most congregations in the African Methodist Episcopal Church, programs have not been developed to enhance the life of women and to prepare them to move into the full life of the church through positions of leadership and authority.

The traditional functions of the Women's Missionary Society of the African Methodist Episcopal Church—queen's contests, teas, fashion shows, workshops, and other fundraising events—are not fulfilling the deep seated needs of the women of African Methodism. While this organization certainly has its place in the church, it is not designed to fulfill the need women have to be mentored by other African-American Christian women. It is imperative, therefore, that women define their own needs and implement programs that will train and prepare them to meet the needs of the larger part of the congregation—women! Our women must be given the opportunity to "come to voice."

Women have been crying unto the Lord for help, for guidance and for affirmation in the body of Christ. All too often women have been made to feel like second class citizens in the body of Christ. Although most churches would not be able to survive spiritually, programmatically or financially without its women, women are not accepted as capable leaders in most of our African American churches.

In all too many churches the female is not welcome in the pulpit. Nor is she asked to serve as deacon, trustee, steward or other major offices in the church. She is expected to follow and not lead; to listen and not speak; to respond when her male pastor preaches and contribute when the offering plate is passed. She is to cook and serve meals in the church, cover her head and sit in the pew and listen uncritically to her male leader who is, in many instances, less educated than she is.

Dr. W. Franklin Richardson, former secretary of the National Baptist Convention, United States of America, Inc., talked about church women's dilemma in the *"Detroit News."*

> Women are the backbone of the church. They have been willing to do the things men haven't wanted to do, yet they haven't received the credit they deserve ... we are just now beginning to understand that sexism is the same (as racism). It doesn't make any sense to train these women as theologians and ministers and not give them a position.[37]

God has responded to the cry of God's women by equipping pastors, both male and female, with the ability to develop programs and ministries that will edify women and equip them to be the *"help meet"* God fashioned her to be in the home, church, community and the world.

Exodus 2:23-25 states:

> *And it came to pass in the process of time, that the King of Egypt died, and the children of Israel sighed by reason of the bondage, and they cried, and their cry came up unto God by reason of the bondage. And God heard their groanings, and God remembered his covenant with Abraham, with Isaac and with Jacob. And God looked upon the children of Israel, and God had respect unto them.*

Just as God heard the Israelites cry, God has heard our cry!

The Bible was our foundation for this Women's Ministry Program. Therefore we examined Scripture as a basis for this undertaking. We soon found that there is "nothing new under the sun." We found our own situations, our own dilemmas, our own pain and joys, and our own story in the lives of biblical women. We found our identities in the stories of Hagar and Sarah, Ruth and Naomi, Vashti and Esther, Rebecca and Leah, Rahab and Bathsheba, Jephthah's daughter, Mary and Martha, the woman at the well, and countless other "certain women." More importantly, we discovered through the Word of God how to handle the situations we face today as we strive to be God's women mentoring other women.

I believe this exercise has provided solid biblical teachings and supportive relationships for women facing the challenge of Godly living in an ungodly world. A church without a women's ministry is an incomplete church. A "Sisters Sharing" ministry will help fill that void. Much prayer and planning must take place in order for "Sisters Sharing" ministries to become a reality in every local church. Women, as well as men, must allow the barriers to come down. We must be willing to "re-think" the Word of God.

Vicki Kraft writes:

> There is a distinct difference between tradition and biblical truth. While the Bible is divine and infallible, tradition is human and fallible. Women and men must learn the difference. Discerning the impact of culture and tradition on the understanding of truth is important in planning how to implement this essential ministry to women.[38]

Women must be carefully and purposefully taught what the Word of God says about who we are as a part of the body of Christ. Then, and only then, will women be able to distinguish cultural teachings from sound theological teachings, and become liberated as a unique part of God's kingdom building agenda.

Women are ready for female mentoring programs. It's time for the church to get ready.

## PERSONAL GROWTH OBSERVATIONS

This project has both challenged and motivated me as a pastor and particularly as a pastor who happens to be female. It has forced me to closely examine the needs of women both in my congregation and from other denominations, and face the fact that the women in our churches are crying out for help.

The women are thirsty for opportunities to dialogue both about biblical stories and their personal lives. The women are silently crying out to be recognized as an intricate part of the body of Christ. They realize that they are more than a "footnote in redemption." They want to take their rightful place not only in the pews, but also in places of leadership.

While four of the women in our "Sisters Sharing" group were aspiring for the preaching ministry (one preached her initial sermon New Year's Eve; one was already preaching and two have not yet preached initial sermons), the majority of the women simply want to serve, to use the gifts and talents they have recognized in their lives to serve the church of the Lord Jesus Christ.

The project challenged me to listen, I mean really listen to the women's stories—stories of pain that comes from rejection, abuse, molestation, loss, depression, divorce, death of a loved one, sickness and loneliness. And as I listened to their stories, I was challenged to do all I could to provide opportunities for healing.

The challenge these women presented—they looked to me as an agent of God for answers—motivated me to work steadfastly with not only this "Sisters Sharing" group, but to help develop groups like ours in any church that would open its doors to the ministry.

We journeyed together for a year—twelve months we were relating, bonding, sharing, trusting, depending and looking to one another for support and encouragement. These twelve months proved to be a turning point in the lives of the women who participated. It is very difficult to measure internal changes except to watch for outward behavioral changes. Even though the leader could listen and hear testimonies of "a brand new me," one cannot adequately transfer those feelings, expressions, tears and smiles onto paper. Even the writings of the women about their understanding of the lessons we covered and their new found understanding of what it means to be a sister and mentor, and to support other women, does not fully express the changes and growth I witnessed having journeyed with these women for the past twelve months. If only hearts could truly be heard.

This project leaves me determined to be a more sensitive pastor—a pastor who will be careful to look beyond the exteriors of the women and the men who sit and listen to me every Sunday morning. I will strive to look past the exterior and seek ways to get to know the people on a heart level, to see where they hurt and what truly brings them joy. The women have forced me to this new level of ministry, and I am grateful to God for each of them. I see them as disciples who will now go and make disciples. They will inevitably share what they have experienced; they will make a difference in the congregations and communities where they serve.

# APPENDIX

## WHERE AM I COMING FROM AND WHERE AM I GOING?

### SHARON

I came into being on October 25, 1945 in a trailer in Fairfield, Maryland. I was the youngest of three children born to a 33 year old woman whose husband was 22 years her senior. My sister is two years older than I. My mother had my brother by a previous marriage and wanted no more children. I could understand that because she was the oldest girl of twelve children; she also had a twin brother. Mom had a hard childhood taking care of all those sibling, working on a farm and not being able to go to school as she wanted.

She probably thought that my father would not want anymore kids either. My father has three children around my mother's age. But, with all of her reminders that, "Your daddy begged me to have you," she loved us.

She was very strict and did not spare the rod. She believed that children should be seen and not heard; she believed every lie a grown-up told on us. I remember my sister getting beatings because a neighbor lied to cover for her child. That saddened me but I understood that mom would never lie on another child, so how could she believe another adult would?

My dad spoiled us rotten. He would sneak candy to us after we were in bed. When mom got on him about disciplining us, he would pretend to beat us with his belt while hitting the quilts, and we would pretend to cry. We were too dumb to let that suffice. We kept being noisy until mom would come with the belt and remove the quilt to hit our raw meat. That's all it took.

I remember a warm day in 1950 when Mom was planning a party for my fifth birthday. It must have been Indian Summer when my headaches began. They were very painful. I got really sick and I remember Mom crying while wrapping me up and taking me back and forth to the doctor. I was admitted eventually to John Hopkins Hospital ... diagnosis: "Polio" or Infantile Paralysis. That is where I spent my birthday. I remember my birthday toy from my Aunt Blanche ... a funny little man that did something mechanically. I remember how I loved that toy and when the polio virus was cured and they transferred me to Children's Hospital School for rehabilitation, they would not let me take it or any of my toys. My heart was broken and I cried relentlessly. They were afraid of spreading polio to my new environment. I thought they were being mean.

From age five through twelve, there were back braces, physical therapy and a hand operation. My spine was curving as a result of Polio, but I did not know that then. I could see that my right shoulder was lower than my left, but I thought it would stay that way. I didn't know it was progressive and surgery was imminent before I stopped growing. Mom was afraid that I would die from the operation and, of course, nobody asked me.

At age twelve, before school closed for summer vacation, Mom and I went to Children's Hospital for my annual checkup. Dr. McDonnell looked at Mom and said, "Well, Mother"? Mom looked sad and told him no. Well, excuse me but what were they talking about? Well, what? As I began to question them, Mom finally told me about the operation to straighten my spine and that she was afraid I would die. Dr. McDonnell showed me my x-ray where my spine looked like a question mark. He explained that by the time I reached adulthood, I would be bent over totally, halfway to the ground. I turned to Mom and asked, "Who's going to marry me like that? I would rather die than be like that!" My statements shocked my mother, but persuaded her to give her consent. We would surgically correct this condition, scoliosis, as soon as school was out.

Surgery was complicated and I missed my entire eighth grade year of school. I did not fail because I had a tutor. I returned to school for ninth grade and was graduated to the tenth grade at Frederick Douglas Senior High School. This was my first normal city school. I went to Francis M. Wood Elementary for handicapped kids for five years. I skipped sixth grade and was graduated to William S. Baer school for seventh grade. I was bused to both of these schools. The city did provide taxi service for me during my senior high school years. People thought my parents were rich to send me to and from school every day for three years in a cab. Of course, I didn't tell them any different. Only my closest friends knew.

I did not do well in tenth grade. It was hard to adjust from two nurturing schools to a school where teachers were cold and impersonal. I became an honor student in grade eleven and remained so until graduation in June 1962.

In September of 1962, I entered Morgan State College at age 16. I went full-time for one and one-half years until I fell in love. I got pregnant, married and dropped out of school in 1964. My husband, Elton Leroy Faulkner, worked at White Coffee Pot Restaurants. We were poor; I did not work. We were not happy. The only joy in my life then was my beautiful little girl, Monique. Lee (Leroy) went to New York where he could make more money. I was returned home to my parents in 1965.

In 1969, I had Elton St. Clair Faulkner. We were so happy. Everyone wanted a boy except Monique; she wanted me to trade him for a girl while at the hospital.

We bought a row house in 1977, and things went well for a while. I tried to make the marriage work but I couldn't do it alone. I hung on, not because my children needed a father, but because I needed someone to do the things that I could not do physically for the kids. When the kids were physically self-sufficient and were driving, I felt that I had had enough. Lee left February 5, 1988, and we were divorced April 4, 1990.

I'm going to become the best computer specialist I can be. I'm going to become healthier by changing my eating habits and getting more rest. I'm going to be a positive influence to everyone, especially my children and granddaughter. I'm going to make sure my granddaughter has everything she needs to become the well-educated, positive, Christian young lady I know God wants her to be. I'm going to buy a home on one level; this will also make me healthier. I'm going to find a husband, with a sense of God, with whom to share my life. I am going to follow a budget because that is the only way I can make sure God gets his ten percent first. I am going to help women understand that putting God first in their lives can help them become self-sufficient and strong enough not to be misused and abused.

Since I put God first in my life, I believe I can accomplish these things while giving God the glory. When God comes "... like a thief in the night." I am going to be, "... caught up to meet Him in the air."

## APRIL

I am a young woman who was raised by grandparents mainly due to having a mother and father who were not ready to be parents. My childhood, at times, was rather painful.

On many occasions, my parents would take me away from my grandparents to live with them. Then, once they couldn't get along, I always ended up back with by grandparents. On a few accounts, my father and mother would fight; then my mother would end up having a nervous breakdown. This went on for some time. Whenever I ended up back with my grandparents, they would involve me in different activities (piano lessons, summer trips, etc.) to help me "get back on track" after the mental abuse from my parents. Basically, my grandparents were all I had to depend on—they were always there for me.

When my parents were not together, they basically didn't have a lot of time for me because they were busy with their own lives. To me it seemed that everything always came before me ... at least other relationships and other kids. Sometimes I wondered if they felt like I wasn't their daughter, or what had I done to them. Later, I realized that there was nothing done wrong on my part. Also, the man to whom my mother would go after breaking up with my father basically abused and controlled her. He didn't allow much communication between us. My mother would sometimes go two or three months before calling me. As for my father's girlfriends, on one hand they liked me and on the other hand, they were jealous of me ... trying to win his attention which, in my opinion, they already had. However, life still continued and my grandparents always tried to make life easier for me; and the way I saw it, they did. This type of lifestyle went on over and over again during my whole childhood.

Then to make life a little more interesting, my grandparents announced that we were moving during the summer before my first year in high school. However, they did allow me to continue to go to the same school. Moving was devastating because the new neighborhood didn't have any kids and was approximately 15 to 20 minutes from my old neighborhood. But I did learn to adjust and now I love it.

During my school years, I was a shy, quiet above average student. When I reached high school, I got into boys. My first boyfriend was probably my worse boyfriend. Unfortunately, when I was going with him I was blindly in love and didn't see the wrong roads he was leading me on, as well as the lies he told. Naturally, my entire family objected to me seeing him (my father even threatened him) which caused a lot of tension between my grandparents and I. But the relationship lasted a few years until finally I had enough; I started seeing other people. The other guys I was seeing didn't really mean much, and I didn't fall in love with any of them. I just had fun with them.

As time went on, I became a Debutante, which was a great honor for me. I went on to graduate from high school. I went to a college that was five minutes from home; began to make new friends and a new lifestyle. While in college, my life changed a lot. I began to grow up more and see life for what it really was. I worked part-time and went to school full-time. I was actively involved in church—as always. However, I knew I was beginning to grow more. My parents still continued in their normal manner; however, I didn't let their problems affect me the way I used to. Things that had been hidden from me as a child came out in the open with my parents. I began to see my mother for who she was, and I realized she put herself into bad situations and then expected me to help her. Today, I still resent the way my mother and father treated me. But thanks to God, I don't hold it against them. I help them when I can; I have never talked bad about them to anyone ... and Lord knows I could have. My father, for the last couple of years, seems to have really gotten his act together. He realizes he can't make up for the lost time, but still tries anyway. I realized that he really loves me but he just didn't know how to show it. My mother is trying to do better; however, she is still traveling on some rough roads. I continue to pray for both of them and ask God to keep a watchful eye over them.

Meanwhile, I finally met someone with whom I really fell in love. With him, I learned the true meaning of the word LOVE. We have a great relationship ... not perfect, but close! He basically came from a "Beaver Cleaver family" where everything was pretty much simple and perfect. He went to the best schools; and his parents made good money and supplied a good life for him. He is my best friend as well as my lover. I truly feel as though God sent him to me, We have grown together in so many ways, spiritually and mentally.

I will be married June 11, 1994. I want to move in a direction where I can continue to get closer to God. I need to learn to trust and depend on Him more. I need to stop the habit of praying about something and then taking the burden back instead of leaving it with God. God has brought me a mighty long way, for which I am truly thankful. I pray that God will make me the wife he would have me to be. I know it won't be easy; however, I know that with the love my fiancee and I have for each other and the love we have for God, it will work.

As for a career, I'm presently praying on whether it is time for me to move on to something else. I don't want to get locked in and be in the same position ten to twenty years from now.

Mentally, I pray that God will remove my unappealing qualities and make me a better person. At the age of 24, I still have a lot of ideas and uncertainties about where I'm going; however, I just pray that God will keep me on the path of his choice and not mine. I also hope that I can some day be an example for someone to help them be where they need to be.

## PATRICIA

Out of my mother's womb came I, naked and a creature ready for God's plan ... at least that is what I would like to think.

Attending church was and still is second nature to me. As a child, my grandmother ("Ma") made sure that Sunday always included Sunday School and worship services, no matter how long they were. I attended first out of obedience to grandmother, who looked so pleased when I was out of my grungy jeans and in a clean crisp dress with patent leather shoes shining, hair held in place with a million (only an exaggeration) barrettes, and even smelling like a girl. I loved Sunday School, because that's where I first met Him. Oh, He took my heart at our first encounter. He knew exactly what to say to convince me that I was His and He was mine. That is where I first met my love, Jesus.

As I matured physically, my spiritual growth dwindled. I became distracted with earthly pleasures and the opposite sex. No longer did I view my spiritual growth as the basic foundation for my overall maturity, I treated life as an entertainment; fun, fun, fun was all that was on my mind. Early in my life I had a dream of becoming a school teacher. As I progressed in my physical and mental existence, my aspirations changed. At one point, I had forgotten my early objective and embarked upon a journey that has continued, even unto this day.

I messed up ... If I would put every relationship in a hat, shook the hat up and pulled out one at random, it would read the same ... I messed up. If I were to put every conscious effort that I have attempted in a hat, shook that hat up and pulled one out at random, it would read the same ... I messed up!!!

Messing up had become a way of life. I would go blindly to the next stage without thought or even an inkling of what or where I was going. I'd end in the same situation, same mode of thinking and without a way out, or so it seemed. Even if I had a period of strict study, service or duty, or sincere effort there I'd be messed up again.

When I graduated from high school, I had planned to enter

the Air Force and pursue a future through rigorous training and disciplined living. In other words, let somebody else tell me how to live and feel, without giving the matter a second thought. Two points prevented that dream, that hope of discovery.

I sulked for about four months. Within that time I met my husband and agreed to marry him with hopes of at least accomplishing something positive in my life. As I struggled through my marital existence, I realized that those two points had cost me the expense of my self esteem; somehow I had to regain it.

I always had an urgency to fit in, to be part of a family, to have a harmonious family unit, to be known as a correct and fitting part of a working unit. Trying so hard to fit, I became a misfit. I always felt that way until Ma put her arms around me and told me everything was going to be alright and that she loved me. But Ma is gone, and has been since May 29, 1979.

When I married in 1973, I truly believed that my husband was my best friend. I could tell him anything. I would sit on his lap and just talk about the smallest to the biggest problem I was having. Everything that was a major concern to me (at least in my mind it was major as well as disturbing), I was able to tell him. I shared my fears of not feeling really loved by my father, being uneasy about not knowing who my biological mother was, unsure about whether I'd ever conceive and give birth, and have a working relationship with him. But then something happened; that trust was violated.

I drifted after my divorce; it took a constant battle to keep my sanity. I was unable to focus upon the divine plan God had for my life, or even remember what that plan might have been. I found myself reluctantly preparing for Sunday service. It all seemed boring to me, a chore instead of a pleasurable time to become reacquainted, reintroduced, or able to bathe in God's glory at the end of a most trying week. I found myself daydreaming during worship, with the hope of getting through it very quickly. I wanted it to end as quickly as possible so that I could go to the next phase. I had the attitude: "at least I came."

I often confused myself with thoughts of what it is that I'm searching for. I haven't found it yet. I can't seem to put my finger on it. Each time I'm asked to perform a task that involves creative thinking, I ask myself should I pursue this road? Maybe I could write a book about my life ... but then there are a zillion of those on the shelf now about famous people. I always had the idea of starting my own business, one that would require my gifts, to use them in a way that would glorify God my Creator.

I find myself looking for my place in life. I've been looking for a long time. I have felt that I was getting closer, but somehow the directional signs were moved, and each road I take has been a dead end so far. Detours don't count; they only cause you to go in circles and get back on the same road.

Along the way, I sort of reconstructed God's plan for my life. I began creating, haphazardly of course, my own happiness. I thought I was really enjoying myself. I drank as much whisky as my belly could hold; I smoked as much reefer as my lungs could hold; I tried to snort up half of South America; and men were at an unlimited number. Wow! At this point I'll pause and thank God for His grace.

The day, the moment, the exact second I was reintroduced to Jesus, I began a brand new journey in my walk. I will not be so presumptuous to say that I have perfected my walk, just that I am a lot more conscious about where and how I must walk. I have better vision, which gives me hope each day. And I thank my pastor, Reverend Ann Lightner for holding that door open for me through Christ Jesus.

Have you ever met somebody again for the first time. A commercial comes on the television set advertising Kellogg's Corn Flakes; I think of it every time I think if the goodness of Jesus, and all that he has done for me. It was like a breath of fresh air. Our meeting again was an encounter that did not proceed a sordid affair; it didn't incorporate the re-living of our first meeting, but allowed a brand new beginning that gets better and better with each day. You see, Jesus gave me a start and a different point of view of my life. I find myself thinking of ways to serve Him better, instead of waiting for someone to tell me how to serve Him. I only want to be what He would have me to be in order for Him to give me that ultimate assignment to complete. Serving Him isn't a task or a begrudging duty, as I once viewed it; it is complete in an excellent way.

When my reintroduction to Jesus happened I was in a transitory state. I was only existing, participating in living and I had no purpose ... You know the song. I had decided: "Okay, I'll go to church, sit through worship and come out feeling no different, but at least I went." But when I was introduced, via Reverend Ann, I discovered that for true and for real Jesus loves me. I was given hope and a new way to serve that brings me sheer delight. Even when I find myself disappointed in what goes on around me, the disgruntled church member, the unhappy and unfulfilled board member, every reason to quit, I think about my best friend who never gives up; I think about Jesus.

Since my new relationship with Jesus, I have grown in a new direction. Being associated with my beloved pastor, I have been granted the opportunity to be introduced to workshops, women's Bible studies, special worship services and retreats that aid in building me up spiritually. I have regained my self-esteem and use my strength and knowledge to encourage others.

Where Am I Going? No place but up. I feel myself rising everyday, even when it may seem to be turning into an awful day, my victory is in Jesus. I'm going up because up is where my spirit has been pointed since the beginning of my existence. And besides, up is where Jesus and Ma is.

## KAREN

I was born to young parents, my mother was 18 and my father was 24. My parents eloped before I was born, and when I turned two years old, the three of us moved to Albany, New York. We remained in New York for nine years, then moved back to Baltimore.

Looking back, I see that although my parent's marriage had its ups and downs, they had happier times in Albany than in Baltimore. Also, as a family we had better times in Albany. The move back to Baltimore may have been financially sound for my father, but it was a giant step backwards for my mother.

My mother is a strong-willed person. When things get her down, she finds the energy to put matters into perspective and do what she has to do to prevail. I admire that quality in her.

When I turned five years old, I was sent to Baltimore for the summer to stay with my grandparents; that tradition remained until we moved back to Baltimore. Every Sunday I was in church from Sunday School through morning service. In Albany, my family probably went to church for one year of all the nine years we were there. I loved Sunday school, and I can remember going to Sunday school the last year we were in Albany. When we moved back to Baltimore, the summer tradition of attending church with my grandmother became a regular weekly tradition (my grandfather was now deceased). My parents did not go to church with us every Sunday, but they would go for special occasions, like the times I sang in the choir for Thanksgiving Day, when I was in an Easter play, when I was baptized, and when I joined the Missionaries.

I stopped attending the church I was raised in, on a regular basis, once I was in college. The four years I lived with my boyfriend, now husband, I did not attend church at all. I missed not attending church, so every now and again my mother and I would visit a different church. I never went back to the church I grew up in because I had never really felt close to anyone.

When my daughter was born, I vowed that I would find a church to call home. When my daughter was 22 months old, I found Mt. Calvary Church, and instantly I knew this was where I belonged.

I've re-dedicated my life to Christ and I am striving to be the best Christian I can. When God looks down at me, I want Him to be proud of who He sees. All the years that I belonged to the other church, I believed that yelling, shouting and jumping up out of your seat once you have received the Holy Ghost was undignified. I told my grandmother that no one will ever see me doing that. But now, after one year of attending Mt. Calvary, I see people receiving the Holy Ghost in a brand new light. There is nothing undignified about it.

At present, I am 29 years old and my marriage is falling apart. My husband, who was not raised in the church, cannot understand my re-dedication to Christ. All he can see is that church is taking me away from him. To him church should be taken in moderation. By attending church every Sunday, going to Bible Study on Wednesday nights, once a month Sister Sharing, and being involved in the young children's choir is taking too much of my time away from him. I keep telling him that I am doing what makes me happy. He keeps telling me that I am going to church myself to death, and that I put him last. Do you want to hear something funny? When my husband was on a softball league last spring, he chose to play Wednesday evenings and Sunday morning games. He would ask me to come watch him play ball, and when I'd tell him that I was going to church, he would get an attitude. The few times I did go out to see him play, he would get on my nerves because he expected me to watch our two year old daughter and him at the same time. So, of course, when he hit a home run and I did not see it, because I was chasing after our daughter, he would become hostile towards me.

I am glad I rededicated my life to Christ when I did; I am really going to need his infinite wisdom and spiritual knowledge to keep my mind clear and focused on what seems to be inevitable in my marriage, a separation or a divorce.

## URSULA

I was an only child but I was raised in the same household with my mother, my natural grandparents and my five cousins.

My parents were divorced when I was very young. I only remember my father visiting me on the holidays. As I got older I remember receiving the child support checks from my father and using them on anything I wanted.

I never knew what it was to have a dominant male in my life when I was young. My grandfather and great-grandfather spoiled me rotten. I had a happy childhood and was taught "the sky is the limit."

When I finished high school, I won a scholarship. All I could think was that I was in love and wanted to get married. I found out later that my mother was upset because I didn't go to college and become a teacher like her.

I got married young and had a baby. My husband and I were from different worlds. He believed a woman's place was in the home. I was independent and wanted to do things when I wanted. When my daughter was two years old, I announced to my family that I was going to look for a job. Oh, how everyone laughed at me. This gave me more determination.

I found that job after three weeks. Maybe this was my downfall. I began going out with the girls. My husband was a good provider and dedicated to his job, not giving me any time to be with him. We separated. I went back to live with my grandmother. I dated many men. I had a tendency to date weak men. These men always gave me my way.

My husband and I went to counseling; he wanted to try again. My mind was made up not to try. I finally filed for divorce. My daughter and I moved into our own apartment.

I got tired of the dating scene and rededicated my life to Christ. I became totally involved in my family and church. I worked and spent time with the family. Others may call it dull, but I felt I was satisfied. One evening while out celebrating my girlfriend's birthday, I met someone new. We talked and dated on and off for many years. This man was different than any I had been involved with. He was strong, dominant and had some of the same ideals I had. We bought a home and later married (backwards, but this is how it happened). Was I always lacking this type of male presence in my life? I often wonder.

After 30 years, my father and I have renewed our relationship. He has asked for forgiveness for not being there when I was growing up.

I came from being a spoiled brat to becoming a woman that puts God first in everything and appreciates his blessings. I'm striving to be a woman that will make a difference in the lives of some of the people I come into contact with daily. I'm striving to be the kind of wife that shows love and patience to a man that knew me when, and to let him know that it was nothing but the grace of God that made me who I am today. I'm striving to be the kind of parent that my child knows she can count on. I'm striving to be the kind of mother-in-law that not only talks forgiveness and understanding, but shows it. I'm striving to be the kind of grandmother that will not spoil her grandchildren to the point that others can't stand to be around them and they will become brats like I was. I'm striving to be the kind of daughter that will make my parents proud.

## YOLONDA

I come from New York City—a city filled with anything you want, anytime you want it. I am a daughter of a numbers running father and a welfare mom. My parents are not now, nor ever were in a positive loving relationship. I am, simply put, the result of a purely physical relationship. Dad's influence in my life has been nil. Mom is the one who made sure I did the right thing.

My life had been one of physical and spiritual poverty. We lived in a mice and drug infested building. The neighborhood was designed to keep you down. Living in a neighborhood filled with so much negative energy, it is hard to maintain a positive attitude. It is easy to think of yourself as a failure. My mother did not get out of the neighborhood. However, she made sure I did. She made sure I knew there was a life outside of Crown Heights. What she didn't give to herself, she gave to me.

Now the question is where am I going? Fear is a strong opponent. I have come a good way from the corners of St. Johns and Classon. I no longer have to live with mice and drugs. I don't have to live with abusive men. So why have I stalled my own progress? Fear! Fear that tells me you ain't nothing but that ghetto girl; fear that tells me I can't achieve my goals.

Back to the original question, "Where am I going?" I am going up. I am going to destroy that fear demon. Where I'm going is not so much a place as a mind set. I am going to achieve positive thinking for myself. I am going towards excellence for me. I am going to love myself. I am going to be the person God wants me to be.

# *ENDNOTES*

[1] Renita Weems, Just A Sister Away (San Diego, California: LuraMedia, 1988), viii.

[2] C. Eric Lincoln and Lawrence Mamiya, The Black Church in the African-American Experience (Durham, N.C.: Duke University Press, 1990), 275.

[3] Religious Experiences and Journal of Mrs. Jarena Lee, "A Preach'in Woman", AMEC Sunday School Union/Legacy Publishing, Nashville, Tennessee, p. 13.

[4] Ibid.

[5] Ibid., iv.

[6] Excerpt from Sojourner Truth's, "Ain't I A Woman" Speech at the 1851 Woman's Rights Convention in Akron, Ohio.

[7] The Detroit News. August 9, 1992, 6A.

[8] Lincoln and Mamiya, 274.

[9] Ibid.

[10] Lincoln and Mamiya, 275.

[11] Patricia Hill Collins, Black Feminist Thought (New York, N.Y.: Routledge, 1990), 22.

[12] Ibid.

[13] Ibid.

[14] Bell Hooks, Talking Back (Boston: South End Press, 1989), 16.

[15] Ibid., 29.

[16] Herbert Lockyer, All The Women In The Bible (Grand Rapids: Zondervan Publishing House, 1967), 190.

[17] Theme from Trinity United Church of Christ, Chicago, Illinois, Dr. Jeremiah A. Wright, Pastor

[18] It was in the "upper room" that the disciples and the women waited for the promise of the Holy Ghost to fall on them. Their lives were totally changed because of the empowering of the Holy Spirit. (Acts 2:1)

[19] Aida Besancon Spencer, Beyond The Curse (New York: Thomas Nelson Publishers, 1985), 56.

[20] The A.M.E. Church Review, October/December, 1992.

[21] Leon-Desour,Xavier, Dictionary of Biblical Theology (New York: Seabury Press) 1973), 72.

[22] Samuel S. Wesley, "The Church's One Foundation," A.M.E. Hymnal (Nashville: A.M.E. Church, 1954), 375.

[23] Collins, 96.

[24] Ibid., 24.

[25] Ibid., 96,97.

[26] Ibid., 87.

[27] Mary C. Lewis, Herstory: Black Female Rites of Passage (Chicago: Africa American Images, 1988), 10.

[28] Weems, 12-13.

[29] Langston Hughes, Selected Poems Langston Hughes (New York: Vintage Books, 1974), 187.

[30] Compilation Committee, eds., African Methodist Episcopal Church: The Book of Discipline (Nashville: AMEC Publishing House, 1988), 19-22.

[31] Ibid., 27.

[32] Ibid., 27-33.

[33] Ibid.

[34] Webster's Third New International Dictionary of the English Language (Unabridged) (Springfield: MA, G & C Merriam Co., 1991), 2128.

[35] Weems, viii.

[36] Ibid., ix.

[37] Ibid., 6A.

[38] Vicki Kraft, Women Mentoring Women, (Chicago, Illinois: Moody Press, 1992), 15.

# ANNOTATED BIBLIOGRAPHY

Abatso, George and Yvonne, How to Equip the African American Family, Urban Ministries, Inc., Chicago, Illinois, 1991.

> *Contains issues and guidelines for building strong families. Writing with psychology and education backgrounds, the authors explore avenues for developing strong Black families in spite of societal pressures. Contains guidelines for strengthening both the single parent, dual parent and extended African-American family. Each chapter contains case studies and Bible study applications.*

Asante, Molefi Kete, Kemet, Afrocentricity and Knowledge, African World Press, Inc., Trenton, New Jersey, 1990.

> *The author addresses the most important theoretical question facing the discipline of African-American studies. Asante's point is that Africology is a discipline, not a group of courses related only to their subject matter.*

Asante, Molefi and Kariamu Welsh, African Culture The Rhythms of Unity, African World Press, Inc., Trenton, New Jersey, 1990.

> *Essays by a collection of 13 authors known as important voices in the African world to discuss commonalities and similarities in African culture. Attempts to lift the fog cast over cultural understanding of the African people by western and western trained scholars in their limited knowledge of African culture.*

Bell, Derrick A., Race, Racism, And American Law, Little Brown & Company, New York, New York, 1973.

> *The author examines several law cases involving minorities and discrimination in the American Law System. Shows that justice is not blind and that Blacks and other minorities in America still face racism in the courts of this country.*

Ben-Jochannan, Yosef A.M., African Origins of the Major "Western Religions", Black Classic Press, Baltimore, Maryland, 1970.

*A critical examination of the history, beliefs and myths which are the foundation of Judaism, Christianity and Islam. The African influences and roots of these religions are highlighted.*

Brown, Cheryl Anne, No Longer Be Silent, Westminster/John Knox Press, Louisville, Kentucky, 1992.

*The author provides a descriptive analysis of the portrayals of several women biblical figures - Deborah, Jephthah's daughter, Hannah and the witch of Endor, in biblical antiquities and Jewish antiquities and contrasts those portrayals by Philo and Josephus.*

Bryant, Cecelia-Williams, Kiamsha, Akosua Visions, Baltimore, Maryland, 1989.

*Author prescribes a spiritual discipline for African- American women, mostly in the form of poetry.*

Champion, G.L. Sr., Black Methodism Basic Beliefs, The African Methodist Episcopal Church Publishing House, Nashville, Tennessee, 1980.

*The author uses a "catechismic format" in presenting categories of all beliefs of all Black methodists. A tool for training methodists about their beliefs and mission. The study is designed for youth probationers, lay persons and clergy of the Methodist Church.*

Champion, G. L. Sr., Christian Education for The African American Church, Broadway Printing Company, Inc., West Palm Beach, Florida, 1990.

*A Christian education manual designed to promote church growth through the Sunday School, both youth and adult. Dr. Champion's manual speaks to multiple ministries in the church including singles, seniors and African-American men with an end to strengthening the body of Christ through the taught Word of God.*

Christenson, Evelyn, Lord, Change Me!, Victor Books, Wheaton, Ill., 1989.

*Teaches women how to change personal attitudes and control outside negative forces that are designed to destroy the spiritual woman. Encourages looking at self for change rather than expecting change in others.*

Clark, Reginald M., Family Life and School Achievement: Why Poor Black Children Succeed or Fail, The University of Chicago Press, Chicago, Illinois, 1983.

*A study of Black family life to examine the wide variation of academic achievement among children. Clark contends that family culture is the most important indication of academic potential, not family structure or income. Offers suggestions and strategies for use by teachers, parents, school administrators and social service policy makers.*

Coleman, Paulette, Editor., The A.M.E. Review, Published quarterly by authority of the Board of Publication of the A.M.E. Church, Nashville, Tennessee, 1993.

*A collection of scholarly religious articles written primarily by ministers and lay persons from the A.M.E. Church as well as other denominations.*

Collins, Patricia Hill, Black Feminist Thought, Rutledge, Chapman and Hall, New York, 1991.

*The author investigates the words and ideas of Black feminist intellectuals as well as the African-American woman outside academe. Under the theme of coming to voice, the author encourages Black females to take control of their own lives. She explores the themes of oppression, family, work and activism as well as new areas of cultural thinking about Black men and women in this century.*

Diop, Cheikh Anta, Civilization or Barbarism: An Authentic Anthropology, Lawrence Hill Books, Brooklyn, New York, 1981.

*Diop offers a critical challenge to orthodox scholarship's interpretation of Egypt as a white civilization, which arose during the nineteenth century to reinforce European racism and imperialism. Amassing evidence from the linguistic to the archaeological, from the historical to the philosophical, he demonstrates that Egypt was a Black civilization and that Blacks are the rightful heirs to Egypt's proud legacy. Shows that Greek civilization, long revered as the birthplace of western thought, owes a substantial debt to Egyptian ideas and accomplishments.*

Diop, Cheikh Anta, <u>The African Origin of Civilization Myth or Reality</u>, Chicago Review Press, Inc., 1974.

*This work of the late Mr. Diop, edited and translated by Mercer Cook, presents the thesis that historical archeological and anthropological evidence supports the theory that civilization of ancient Egypt, the first that history records, was actually Negroid in origin.*

Giddings, Paula, <u>When and Where I Enter</u>, Bantam Books, New York, New York, 1984.

*Describes the impact of Black women on race and sex in America from the 17th century to today. Utilizes speeches, diaries, letters and other original sources.*

Gillman, Florence M., <u>The Women Who Knew Paul</u>, The Liturgical Press, Collegeville, Minnesota, 1992.

*An exploration of the lives of women who were introduced by Paul and known primarily in connection with Paul. The author brings these women out of Paul's shadow and gives the reader a personal account of their lives.*

Hale-Benson, Janice E., <u>Black Children: Their Roots, Culture and Learning Styles</u>, The Johns Hopkins University Press, Baltimore, Maryland, 1986.

*Emphasizes the significance of culture and cultural experience upon the development and educational advancements of African-American children in the United States. Seeks to find ways of improving the effectiveness of educational programs geared toward Black children.*

Hart, Thomas N., <u>The Art of Christian Listening</u>, Paulist Press, New York, Ramsey, 1980.

*Prepares the Christian helper to better understand his or her role, and to comprehend the objectives and limits of those roles. Shows the many ways in which we can serve others by listening to their stories.*

Hayford, Jack, <u>Rebuilding The Real You</u>, Regal Books, Ventura, California, 1986.

*Explores the work of the Holy Spirit in the book of Nehemiah and how the Holy Spirit works to bestow believers from brokenness. Demonstrates the believer's ability, to rise above that which cripples us.*

Hicks, Ingrid D., <u>For Black Women Only: A Complete Guide to A Successful Life-Style Change, Health, Wealth, Love and Happiness</u>, African-American Images, Chicago, Illinois, 1991.

*A self-help book written for Black women. Black women tell their own success stories about experiences as wives, mothers, daughters, friends, workers and entrepreneurs.*

Hoffman, Jo Ann, <u>Churches In Solidarity With Women-1992-1993 Yearbook</u>, A.M.E. Publishing House, Nashville, Tennessee, 1993.

*A study guide for the Women's Missionary Society and Young People's Division for the connectional A.M.E. Church. Designed to help address questions regarding women in the A.M.E. Church, to the end that discrimination against women, who comprise the larger body of the church, will be rooted out through education.*

Hollies, Linda J., Editor, <u>Womanistcare: How To Tend the Souls of Women, Volume I</u>, WTWMI Publications, Joliet, Evanston, Illinois, 1992.

*African-American women tell their own stories and express the need to be cared for by pastoral care-givers. The nine writers are ordained, seminary educated, clinically trained women who collaborate to bring into consideration a new view of pastoral care and counseling.*

Hooks, Bell, <u>Ain't I A Woman</u>, South End Press, Boston, Mass., 1981.

*Examines the impact of sexism on Black women during slavery, the historic devaluation of Black womanhood, Black male sexism, racism within the women's movement, and the Black woman's involvement with feminism.*

Hooks, Bell, Talking Back, South End Press, Boston, Massachusetts, 1988.

*A liberating message about thinking feminist, thinking Black. Encourages women to speak their mind on issues concerning women. Purports that there is power in the spoken word.*

Hull, Bill, The Disciple Making Pastor, Fleming H. Revell Company Publishers, Tarrytown, New York, 1988.

*The author calls pastors to take a serious look at the lack of discipleship ministries in the local church. This work focuses on the importance of commitment to this vital task to the end that pastors will build healthy Christians who are ready to obey Christ's mandate to make disciples.*

Jakes, T.D., Woman Thou Art Loosed!, Destiny Image Publishers, Shippensburg, Pennsylvania, 1993.

*A collection of fifteen messages designed to liberate the mind, body and soul of women. An in-depth view of the lives and circumstances of the biblical women.*

Karenga, Maulana, Selections From The Husia, Sacred Wisdom of Ancient Egypt, The University of Sankore Press, Los Angeles, California, 1984.

*The Husia (coming forth by Day) provides a brief representative selection of ancient Egyptian sacred literature which can serve as a readable and enjoyable reference for those interested in ancient Egyptian and African literature in general, whether sacred or secular.*

Kraft, Vickie, Women Mentoring Women, Moody Press, Chicago, Illinois, 1992.

*Explores the need for women ministries in the church and gives detailed guidelines on how to develop ministries for women in the local church.*

Kuenning, Delores, Helping People Through Grief, Bethany House Publishers, Minneapolis, Minnesota, 1987.

*A handbook designed to help persons with a special need to know about a particular kind of grief. True experiences are chronicled with specific suggestions on how to handle different situations where persons are grieving. Includes death, divorce, SIDS, abortion, handicapped children and many more.*

Kunjufu, Jawanza, Critical Issues in Educating African-American Youth (A Talk With Jawanza), African American Images, Chicago, Illinois, 1989.

*A collection of the most challenging questions received by the author since 1974 on issues related to the education of Black youth. The questions relate to teachers and pedagogy, curriculum, learning styles, special education, Black boys, etc.*

Kunjufu, Jawanza, Countering The Conspiracy to Destroy Black Boys, Volumes I, II, and III, African-American Images, Chicago, Illinois, 1982, 1986, 1990.

*Shows the plight of the African-American male and how parents, teachers, administrators, business people and the entire community are a part of the conspiracy to destroy Black males. Shows how the conspiracy can be countered by that same community.*

Lee, Jarena, Religious Experiences and Journals of Mrs. Jarena Lee, A.M.E.C. Sunday School Union, Legacy Publishing, Nashville, TN, 1991.

*Life and labors of the first woman preacher in the A.M.E. Church. Gives her account of her call to preach and the discrimination women suffered in the A.M.E. Church.*

Leon-Dusour, Xavier, Dictionary of Biblical Theology, Seabury Press, New York, New York, 1973.

Lewis, Mary C., HERSTORY Black Female Rites of Passage, African American Images, Chicago, Illinois, 1988.

*Explores the developing adolescent female and explores solutions to teenage pregnancy, school drop-out and healing female relationships. Contains an African Rites of Passage Model for African-American females.*

Lincoln, C. Eric, and Mamiya, Lawrence, <u>The Black Church In The African-American Experience,</u> Duke Univ. Press, Durham, North Carolina, 1990.

*A study of the seven mainline Black denominations in the United States. Authors examine the history of the Black church in America and relates the church to the total African-American experience.*

Lockyear, Herbert, <u>All The Women In The Bible</u>, Zondervan Publishing House, Grand Rapids, Michigan, 1967.

*Author does a categorical study of the women in the Bible, giving details and insight into their various lifestyles, occupations, and achievements.*

Lush, Jean, <u>Emotional Phases of A Woman's Life</u>, Fleming H. Revell Company, Tarrytown, New York. 1987.

*This work explores ways to help women understand and appreciate their emotions. Discusses the relationship between a woman's emotions and her changing physiology.*

MacHappie, Barbara J., <u>Readings in Her Story</u>, Fortress Press, Minneapolis, Minnesota, 1992.

*A collection of primary texts about women in Christianity. This anthology is a collection of 74 important Christian documents and passages by and about women ranging from Genesis to now. Crosses both denominational and gender lines.*

Matthews, Alice, <u>A Woman Jesus Can Teach</u>, Discovery House Publishers, Grand Rapids, Michigan, 1991.

*An exploration of the lives of selected New Testament women and their relationship with Jesus. Designed to help today's women make crucial choices in their lives.*

May, Gerald, Addictions and Grace, Harper Collins Publishers, New York, New York, 1991.

*A psychologist's exploration of the psychology and physiology of addiction. Examines the relationship between addiction and spiritual awareness. Details various addictions from which we can suffer; including work, sex, performance, responsibility, intimacy, drugs and alcohol.*

Menking, Stanley J., Helping Laity Help Others, The Westminster Press, Philadelphia, Pennsylvania, 1984.

*A pastor's handbook defining ministry as the shared responsibility of clergy and congregation. Describes how pastors can help laity fulfill their mission of service. Examples of prayers are given.*

Mohney, Nell W., Don't Put A Period Where God Put A Comma, Dimensions for Living, Nashville, Tennessee, 1993.

*A how to manual on overcoming low self-esteem. Offers biblical guidance for developing a healthy self-esteem. Includes questions for personal reflection and exercises for putting these principles into practice.*

Moore, Maxori, Transformation: A Rites of Passage Resource Manual for African American Girls, STARS Press, New York, New York, 1987.

*A step-by-step instructional book on how to conduct an African-American teenage rites of passage program.*

Myers, William H., The Irresistible Urge To Preach, Aaron Press, Atlanta, Georgia, 1992.

*A collection of eighty six African-American "call" stories of men and women from various denominations involved in significant ministries throughout the United States.*

Norwood, Robin, Women Who Love Too Much, Simon & Schuster, Inc., New York, New York, 1985.

*A self-help guide designed for women in unhealthy relationships. Stories show women in detrimental relationships who took steps to heal or leave the relationship.*

Nwapa, Flora, <u>African Women Writers Series: Women Are Different</u>, African World Press, Inc., Trenton, New Jersey, 1992.

*The author chronicles the lives of a group of Nigerian women from their school days together through the trials and tribulations of their adult lives. Shows the universal problems faced by women everywhere, the struggle for financial independence and a rewarding career, combined with problems of single mothers.*

Ornum, William Van and Mordock, John B., <u>Crisis Counseling With Children and Adolescents</u>, The Continuum Publishing Company, New York, New York, 1988.

*This guide is for non-professional counselors without extensive training who care for troubled children. It covers such traumatic experiences as a death in the family, divorce, sickness, hospitalization, handicaps, aggression and defiance in home and school, and how, if necessary, to make a referral to professional help.*

<u>The Holy Bible</u>

Warfield-Coppock, Nsenga, <u>Afrocentric Theory and Applications, Volume I Adolescent Rites of Passage</u>, Baobab Associates, Inc., Wash., D.C., 1990.

*Introduces the Afrocentric theory and youth development and applies them as steps toward the development of rites of passage programs for adolescents.*

Warfield-Coppock, Nsenga, Afrocentric <u>Theory and Application, Volume I: Adolescent Rites of Passage Training Supplement</u>.

*This training manual was developed to supplement the Volume I book and may be used by professionals and others interested in development of Afrocentric rites of passage programs.*

Webster, Daniel, Webster's Third New International Dictionary of the English Language (Unabridged), G. & C. Merriam Company, Springfield, Massachusetts, 1991.

Weems, Renita J., Just A Sister Away, Lura Media, San Diego, California, 1988.

*Womanist insight into the lives of biblical women, connecting them with women of today. Study questions that follow each chapter provide for soul searching dialogue in which women can grow and develop spiritually.*

Welsing, Frances Cress, The Isis Papers: The Keys to The Colors, Third World Press, Chicago, Illinois, 1991.

*A controversial series of lectures and papers given by author on racism in America.*

Wesley, Samuel S., "The Church's One Foundation," A.M.E. Hymnal, A.M.E. Church, Nashville, Tennessee 1954.

Williams, Chancellor, The Destruction of Black Civilization, Great Issues of a Race From 4500 B.C. to 2000 A.D., Third World Press, Chicago, Illinois, 1987.

*An exploration of Black civilization and the achievements of Blacks independent of Asia or Europe. Explores several questions including: How did all Black Egypt become all White Egypt? How did Africans, among the very first people to invent writing, lose this art almost completely?*

Williams, Delores S., Sisters in The Wilderness, Orbis Books, Maryknoll, New York, 1993.

*A womanist hermeneutic of the Hagar story. Explores the themes inherent in Hagar's story - poverty, slavery, ethnicity and sexual exploitation, exile and encounters with God. Traces parallels in the history of African-American women in slavery to the present.*